Cornish Recipes...
Ancient and Modern

Compiled by Edith Martin

Truro:
Netherton & Worth Ltd., The County Printers.

First published in 1929

This edition published in 2021 by
The Noverre Press

ISBN 978-1-914311-02-4

© 2021 The Noverre Press

PUBLISHER'S NOTE TO THE 2021 EDITION

Many of the recipes in this book would today be considered unsafe, unethical, or dangerous. The publisher therefore stresses that the book should be used only for archival purposes, and the publisher can accept no responsibility whatsoever for any injuries, illnesses, prosecutions, etc. caused by following the recipes herein.

No cormorants were harmed during the production of this book.

PREFACE TO THE FIRST EDITION

In issuing this, the first printed CORNISH RECIPE BOOK, I wish, first of all, to acknowledge with grateful thanks, the very great assistance given me by many members of the Cornish Women's Institutes, members of the Old Cornwall Societies and the public generally.

It is in great part due to their contributions of Recipes, etc., that it has been possible to issue such a fine collection of matter relating entirely to the Duchy of Cornwall.

The collection is probably still incomplete, and should long-forgotten dishes occur to the minds of readers in glancing through this book, I should be glad if they would forward them to me, with any criticisms of this present work, for inclusion or correction in the next edition.

The Recipes have been printed exactly as received, and if it is apparent that there is some slight repetition of the same Recipe it is because it varies in different districts, each of which claims that theirs is the correct one. My readers must judge for themselves.

EDITH MARTIN.

Tregavethan, Truro.
April, 1929.

COMMENDATORY

"*Good wine needs no bush*," *and surely no advertisement is needed for Mrs. Martin's collection of Cornish Recipes, which has run through four editions in six months and is still going (appropriate simile) "like hot cakes." The only discoverable reason for this page then—introducing a fifth and enlarged edition—would seem to be some notoriety achieved by me as a* GOURMET *in Cornish fare. Well, I see no harm in* THAT, *if only the reader will not confuse* GOURMET *with* GOURMAND: *for I despise immoderate eating even more than immoderate drinking; from both of which vices we may claim that the Cornish, preserved perhaps in some measure by their climate, are creditably free. I have known, indeed, a man who could eat a leg of mutton at a sitting, and another who on market-days regularly consumed twenty-four glasses of hot brandy and water before being hoisted into saddle to ride home. But these were survivals from a more granitic age, and I am bound to say that they both died before reaching seventy.*

I have mentioned climate, having learned by observation and experiment that drinks and dishes palatable and health-giving in one country are often unsuitable to others and even pernicious. Simple viands, unhelped by the stock-pot, "belong" to these parts, with light, fermented beverages such as cider and claret. And I wish that our hotels and restaurants in the West would take account of this and discover that visitors to Cornwall (as many of them assure me) enjoy by preference the fare that our mothers and grandmothers took pride in setting on table. I know indeed of one hotel where such fare can always be found, but I shall not name it; in the first place because it is well worth the trouble of searching out, and secondly because it never lacks custom.

As with the viands, so with the cookery. The reader of these pages will observe that most of the recipes given presume a clean hearth and a well swept oven. Would not our visitors at once detect the difference between meat cooked with these simple appliances and the gas cooked dietary of towns? Consider, for example, what a chicken has to suffer anywhere in London. As soon as plucked it has its poor breast broken to make it look plump (a trade trick that any good housewife should resent as an attempted fraud on her intelligence); it is then packed for market in sawdust, the turpentine of which races through its delicate flesh; lastly it is baked in a gas-heated oven wherein the fumes of coal-tar fight it out with the infection already absorbed. That is your townsman's notion of a "roast chicken." It bears no resemblance at all to a Cornish chicken marketed in a clean napkin, seasoned with lemon-thyme and other herbs from the garden, roasted on a spit and thoroughly basted in the process—a "dish to set before the King"—especially when accompanied by home-made bread that has taken the delicate aroma of a furze-heated oven.

I think we shall be grateful to the compiler of the following pages for having rescued so many country recipes and simples in this age of canned foods and "substitutes"; and I propose to show my own gratitude by offering two recipes for her acceptance.

Every well-found house should make it a point of honour to keep a good ham in cut. It is one of the permanent stand-bys of hospitality taken by surprise. Now I know of no better accompaniment for ham, cured as prescribed on page 10, than a few damsons pickled in the following way.

PICKLED DAMSONS.—Take 6 lbs. of damsons sound and dry, and place them in a pan. Boil together 3 lbs. of loaf sugar, 1½ pints of vinegar, ½ oz. of stick of cinnamon, 1 teaspoonful of cloves in a muslin bag. Pour the liquor over the damsons and leave till next day. Then strain off juice, boil up again, pour over fruit, and leave for another day. Then boil all together, put in jars and make airtight.

My other recipe is for a "Cup," which I have mixed with my own hands to gratify some generations of yachtsmen.

'Q'S' CLARET OR CIDER CUP.—To 1 large bottle of sound Claret (or a slightly larger amount of cider) add 1 sherry glass of Cognac; the rind of half a lemon and the pulp in thin slices: a sprig of borage; ice and powdered sugar to taste, but at least one tablespoonful of sugar. Stir twice and then pour in 1 large bottle of Soda Water. Stir again, and according to season, drop in two or three gently pinched strawberries, or half a dozen pinched raspberries or grapes, or a thin slices of English-grown melon. Allow 20 minutes, and stir again before use.

N.B.—*No cucumber, and no lacing with any Liqueur but simple Cognac. A glass jug should be used, any touch of silver of other metal being fatal to wine.*

For a light supper—experto crede—*the above two recipes will be found to help one another very well.*

ARTHUR QUILLER-COUCH.

Fowey,
February, 1930.

INDEX

BEVERAGES	45
BREAD, ETC.	11
CAKES, ETC.	13
CORNISH OVEN, Description of a	72
CREAM	26
CURING HAM AND BACON	10
COMMENDATORY by "Q" (Sir Arthur Quiller-Couch)	4
FISH DISHES	27
MISCELLANEOUS	58
PASTIES	31
PIES	34
PREFACE (by the COMPILER)	3
PUDDINGS	43
REMEDIES (Medical and otherwise)	63
SOUPS AND BROTHS	9
TO A CORNISH RECIPE BOOK (by A. W. JAY) ...	8

[All Recipes are placed in alphabetical order under their classified headings.]

TO A CORNISH RECIPE BOOK

O, Cornwall, with your cliffs so grand,
Your beaches, rich with golden sand;
Where waters blue, and clear, and deep,
By granite boulders silence keep.

Oh, hills and dales, O, valleys green,
A'blaze with heather, seldom seen
Elsewhere than 'midst the Cornish moors,
Or clust'ring round her ancient tors.

Where, bordering road, and path, and lane,
The golden gorse is all aflame,
From early Spring to late September,
As if to pray you to remember

That health abides 'mong Cornish hills,
Where all can find relief from ills;
Where cares and worries of to-day
Will spread their wings and fly away.

And in these pages you will take
Much comfort for your stomach's sake;
For body's ease means rest and quiet,
And here you'll find ideal diet.

Here's Recipes quite polyglot—
Shenagrum, Likky, Eggy'ot,
Star-gazey, Figgy'obben Pie,
And Remedies for Wart and Stye.

There's Cornish Cream and Pasties rare,
And Saffron Cake beyond compare;
So read, mark, learn, digest, and then
Pass on to Tre, and Pol, and Pen.

A. W. Jay.

SOUPS AND BROTHS

A USEFUL FISH SOUP

Take an average sized sized fresh haddock, boil it to shreds in a quart of water, then strain off the stock or liquor and put it into a saucepan, adding at the same time 1 pint of new milk, 1 large onion chopped fine, a small piece fresh butter, and pepper and salt to taste. Simmer the whole till thoroughly cooked and serve up hot. Add a slight thickening if liked. Good for invalids and convalescents.

PERRANPORTH W.I.

Whiting pollack may be used instead of haddock.

CABBAGE BROTH

Take some stock or water that salt beef has been boiled in, cut up small one or two cabbages, boil until tender, then take up in basins, cabbage and all, cut squares of bread, put in basin and eat very hot.

SHORTLANESEND W.I.

"KIDDLEY" BROTH (1)

Bread cut into squares, a few marigold heads, a few stalks of "scifers"* chopped fine, lump of butter, pepper and salt. Put all into a basin, pour boiling water over, and eat as hot as possible.

BOSCASTLE.

"KIDDLEY" BROTH (2)

Boil several onions, strain and put the liquid into a basin with bread cut in squares; butter, pepper and salt to suit taste. Eat very hot.

SHORTLANESEND W.I.

Sometimes called Kettle Broth.

---

* "Scifers" grow all the year round. It is a kind of herb, something like a small shallot, but more grassy looking. The tops only are used.

CURING HAM AND BACON

TO CURE BACON

Dry-salting bacon is best. Mix together 2 lbs. salt, ½ lb. foot sugar, 1 oz. saltpetre. Rub well into bacon, both sides, lay on flat dish, cover with remainder of mixture. Turn daily.

TO CURE HAM BY DRY SALTING

Well rub the skin all over with dry salt, then sprinkle the ham with 2 ozs. saltpetre and 4 ozs. moist sugar, paying special care to the bone by sprinkling a little more immediately around it. Then put into a bussa, cover the whole ham with half-inch thickness dry salt and put into cool place until required for use. The ham should be soaked in cold water for 12 hours before boiling.

TRURO W.I. CENTRE.

TO CURE HAMS OR TONGUES

Take three or four gallons of water, put to it two ounces of Prunella Salt, four pounds of White Salt, four pounds of Bay Salt, a quarter of a pound of Saltpetre, an ounce of Flour, a pound of Brown Sugar, let it boil a quarter of an hour, scum it well; when it is cold, score it from the Bottom into the Vessel you steep it in. Let Ham lie in this Pickle four or five weeks; Tongues a fortnight. Dry them in a Stove or Wood Chimney.

This recipe is dated 1738. TRURO.

TO CURE TONGUE OR BEEF

Ingredients:

- 1 gallon of cold water
- 3 lbs. salt
- ½ lb. pickling sugar
- 1 oz. powdered saltpetre

Method: Boil all together for half an hour; well skim it, then let it go cold before pouring on the tongue or beef. Tongues should be well salted over night, and scraped before putting the cure over.

TRURO W.I. CENTRE.

EVERY COOK PRAISES HER OWN BROTH

BREAD, ETC.

NORTH CORNISH BISCUITS

Ingredients:
   1 lb. flour
   ½ lb. castor sugar
   ½ lb. margarine or butter
   Rather less than an oz. of powdered ammonia

Method: Mix margarine into flour, add sugar and ammonia last. Make into a dough with a little milk, roll out thin, cut in rounds, bake in moderate oven.

MORWENSTOWE W.I.

TO MAKE BREAD

Take 2 ozs. yeast, mix with a teacupful of flour in a basin and make into a smooth paste with ½ pint warm water (*not hot*). Place the basin in a warm place where it will soon work. Weigh 7 lbs. flour into a deep pan and mix with 2 ozs. salt; make a hole in middle of flour and pour in yeast. Mix this well into the flour and add warm water, enough to make a moderately stiff dough. Knead thoroughly for quarter of an hour. This done, place pan in a warm place and when the dough has risen to double, knead again lightly, divide and put into greased tins. Let them rise a short time, and then bake in a hot oven till well browned.

TRURO W.I. CENTRE.

HOME-MADE BREAD

Ingredients:
   7 lbs. flour
   2 ozs. yeast
   1 teaspoonful salt
   Tepid milk and water

Method: Cream the yeast with a little castor sugar, make a well in the centre of the flour, add the yeast and about ½ pint of milk and water, cover over with the dry flour, put in a warm place to rise for 30 minutes. Now work in all the flour, adding more tepid milk and water as may be required. Knead for five minutes, and put into floured tins. Let it rise about 30 minutes. Bake in a steady oven about 1¼ hours.

CALLINGTON W.I.

BREAD IS THE STAFF OF LIFE

BARLEY BREAD

To make the Leaven mix a small quantity of barley flour with warm water into a dough. Form it into a round shape, like a pat of butter; make a dent in the centre with the thumb, about half-way through. Set the dough on a plate, cross it lightly twice, like a hot-cross bun, and fill the dent with warm water. Set it aside for a few days when the dough will have fermented and split like an over-ripe fruit. It is then ready for use instead of yeast to "plum" the bread, which is mixed in the usual way with warm water and a little salt.

When the bread has been sufficiently kneaded, take a small piece of the dough and prepare it for leaven against the next baking day. Cover the newly-mixed bread with a cloth and set in a warm place. When risen, form into cone-shaped loaves and bake under a kettle on the hearth. The loaves were usually grouped in three's, and the soft crust, where the loaves touched each other, was called "kissing crust."

MULLION W.I.

SEEDY BREAD

Take 1 lb. dough, knead in 3 ozs. of lard and a teaspoonful of caraway seeds. Bake in hot oven for 20 minutes.

ST. JUST W.I.

CORNISH SPLITS (1)

Ingredients:
- 1 lb. flour
- 1 oz. butter
- ½ oz. yeast
- ½ oz. castor sugar
- ½ pint tepid milk
- Salt

Method: Cream the yeast and sugar together until they are liquid, then add the milk; sieve the flour and quarter teaspoonful of salt into a basin. Melt the butter gently, add it and the milk, etc., to the flour and mix all into a smoot dough. Put the basin in a warm place, to let the dough rise, for ¾ hour. Then shape it in small round cakes and place them in a floured baking tin. Bake in a quick oven for from 15 to 20 minutes. Split and butter them. Serve very hot. Or may be left until cold, when split and butter them, or split and eat with cream, jam or treacle.

Splits eaten with cream and treacle are known as "thunder and lightning."

TRURO W.I. CENTRE.

HALF A LOAF IS BETTER THAN NO BREAD

BREAD, CAKES, ETC.

CORNISH SPLITS (2)

Ingredients:
- 1 lb. flour
- 2 ozs. lard
- 1 oz. yeast
- ½ pint warm milk
- A good pinch of salt

Method: Prepare yeast in the usual way, rub fat in flour, add salt and mix in the milk gradually, lastly add the yeast. Give the dough a good kneading and put to rise; when risen sufficiently turn out on board dusted with flour, and cut into rounds, and put on baking sheath, put again to rise and then bake in a quick oven until bottoms are brown.

TRURO W.I. CENTRE.

CORNISH SPLITS (3)

½ lb. flour, pinch of salt, pinch of baking powder, mix with butter-milk, roll out and bake in hot oven.

ST. JUST W.I.

CAKES, ETC.

BLACK CAKE (1)

Ingredients:
- ½ lb. flour
- ½ lb. ground rice
- ¾ lb. butter
- ¾ lb. castor sugar
- 2 lbs. currants
- ½ lb. lemon peel
- ½ lb. orange peel
- ¼ lb. chopped raisins
- ¼ lb. chopped sultanas
- ½ lb. chopped almonds
- 1 dozen eggs
- 1 teaspoonful ground spice
- 1 nutmeg
- ½ teaspoon carbonate soda
- 2 teaspoons cinnamon
- 1 teaspoon baking powder
- 2/- brandy

ALMOND PASTE.
- ½ lb. ground almonds
- ½ lb. castor sugar
- 1 egg

ICING.
- ½ lb. icing sugar
- White of one egg

Bake about three hours.

REDRUTH W.I. CENTRE.

This recipe has been used in a Cornish family for many generations. Several cakes are made from above ingredients; one is always kept twelve months and eaten on its birthday, when the new batch is made for the coming year.

YOU CANNOT EAT YOUR CAKE AND HAVE IT TOO

BLACK CAKE (2)

Ingredients:

½ lb. flour
½ lb. fine sugar
¼ lb. lemon peel
¼ oz. cinnamon
3 eggs
1 lb. currants
Bake 4 hours.

¼ lb. butter
2 ozs. citron
1 nutmeg
½ teaspoon of carbonate of soda dissolved in warm milk

PORTSCATHO W.I.

CHRISTMAS CAKE

Ingredients:

½ lb. flour
½ lb. butter
1½ lbs. currants
6 eggs
½ lb. castor sugar
1 wineglassful brandy

2 teaspoonsful carbonate soda
¼ lb. peel
1¼ tablespoonsful vinegar
¼ lb. sweet almonds
Salt

Method: Mix flour, soda, and salt together. Work the butter well into it. Add currants, chopped almonds, peel and sugar. Mix well and add eggs, brandy and vinegar (well beaten). Bake in slow oven for 3 hours.

THE ALMOND PASTE FOR ABOVE.

1 lb. icing sugar, ¼ lb. ground almonds, flavouring, white of one egg, beaten to a stiff froth. Mix well with a knife to a stiff paste, and spread on cake with a silver knife warmed in hot water.

TRURO W.I. CENTRE.

CORNISH FAIRINGS

Ingredients:

6 lbs. flour
3 lbs. raw sugar
2 lbs. butter
½ lb. lard
1¾ lb. lemon peel
3 lbs. syrup

3 ozs. carb. soda
1½ ozs. tartaric acid
½ oz. powdered ammonia
1¼ ozs. ground ginger
1½ ozs. mixed spice

Method: Rub down fat with the flour fine. Mix spices, ammonia, and ginger with above, also sugar. Make a bag to receive syrup. Put soda into half a gill water in a saucepan and just bring to the boil, then pour into syrup.

LITTLE STICKS KINDLE A GREAT FIRE

CAKES, ETC.

Do the same with the tartaric acid. Then stir soda and acid into the syrup until the whole becomes a froth, then mix all together, adding the lemon peel. Mix into a very soft paste and roll out into strips about an inch thick and cut off in pieces about an inch long. Place on greased sheath, bake in a warm oven. If they should run together, mix more flour with the dough.

The mixture may be rolled out about half-inch thick, and cut with a small round cutter, leaving room on the sheath for the biscuits to spread.

LOSTWITHIEL W.I.

CORNISH HEAVY CAKE (1)

Ingredients:

- 1½ lbs. flour
- ¼ lb. butter or cream
- ¼ lb. beef dripping or good lard
- 2 dessertspoons sugar
- 1 teaspoon salt
- Small bit of lemon peel
- ¾ lb. currants

Method: Don't put the butter and lard too fine in the flour; after it is mixed with water roll it out and then roll it up and put it aside for an hour or two, then roll it out again, cut across with knife, the cake will then be light and shaley. Time for baking 20—30 minutes according to size.

FALMOUTH W.I. CENTRE.

CORNISH HEAVY CAKE (2)

Ingredients:

- 1 lb. flour
- ½ lb. grated suet
- 2 ozs. sugar
- 1 oz. peel
- Pinch of salt
- 2 teaspoons baking powder
- ¼ lb. currants

Method: Mix together with milk or butter-milk. Roll out to about ½ inch thickness, cut in rounds, or put on baking sheath, and lightly mark in fair sized squares with knife. Bake in hot oven.

ST. MAWGAN W.I.

CORNISH HEAVY CAKE (3)

Ingredients:

- 1 lb. flour
- 1 lb. fresh butter
- 6 ozs. currants
- Pinch of salt

A LITTLE POT IS SOON HOT

Method: Take ¼ lb. butter and rub into the flour, make it into a stiff dough with cold water; having added the currants and salt, roll it out on the board, take another ¼ lb. butter and lay it in small pieces over the dough, flour and fold it up, roll again twice, adding the remainder of the butter, then roll it out finally an inch thick; score the surface in small diamonds, brush over with milk and bake for half an hour in a quick oven.

MITHIAN W.I.

CORNISH HEAVY CAKE (4)

Ingredients:

1 pint of flour Pinch of salt
1 pint of cream 1 egg, beaten well
½ lb. currants

Method: Mix all together, roll out and bake.

TRURO W.I. CENTRE.

INGREDIENTS FOR A GREAT CAKE

5 lbs. butter brought to a cream Peel of 2 oranges
5 lbs. flour Pint of canary
3 lbs. white sugar ½ pint rosewater
7 lbs. currants 43 eggs (half ye whites)
2/6 worth perfume 1 lb. citron

ST. MAWGAN W.I.

Sent by a St. Mawgan member, culled from an old Cookery Book, dated 1763.

A PENZANCE CAKE

Ingredients:

1 lb. flour ½ oz. ground cinnamon
1 lb. currants 2 eggs
½ oz. ginger A teaspoonful baking-soda
¼ lb. peel dissolved in a cup of warm
¼ lb. butter milk

Method: Cream the butter in the flour and mix in the dry ingredients. Beat the eggs well and stir in with wooden spoon, then the milk. . Bake 2½ to 3 hours in a slow oven.

POLKERRIS W.I.

HE THAT WILL STEAL AN EGG WILL STEAL AN OX

CAKES, ETC.

PIE CAKE

Pastry is made with suet and lard. Cut fresh meat in small pieces, add new potatoes, turnips and onions; roll pastry in two rounds, place vegetables and meat on larger, add salt and pepper, place second round of pastry over and pinch edges together. Cut a small slit in centre of the top.

St. Just W.I.

PORTER CAKE

Ingredients:
- 2 eggs
- ½ lb. butter
- ¾ lb. sugar
- 1½ lb. currants
- ½ teaspoonful mixed spice
- Heaped teaspoonful carbonate soda
- ½ pint stout (porter) warmed

Method: Melt butter, don't allow to boil. Add sugar, add porter, add eggs which must be well beaten. Add flour and sugar together. Add all ingredients and mix for about ten minutes. Bake in two or three small tins in a very moderate oven. Time 2 to 2½ hours.

Tresillian W.I.

This cake will keep for a very long time.

FUGGAN (1)

Ingredients:
- 2 cups of flour
- Pinch of salt
- 2 ozs. of fat (suet, lard)
- Handful of currants

Method: Mix with sour milk or butter milk, roll an inch thick in an oval shape, mark with a knife criss-cross and bake for half an hour.

St. Just W.I.

FUGGAN (2)

Ingredients:
- ½ lb. flour
- 2 ozs. lard
- Pinch of salt
- Handful of raisins

Method: Rub fat in flour, mix with salt and raisins; mix all to a stiff dough with a little water, roll oval shape, and cut acros with a knife.

Madron W.I.

TOO MANY COOKS SPOIL THE BROTH

MEATY FUGGAN

Ingredients:
    2 cups flour   2 ozs. fat
    Pinch of salt

Method: Mix with water, roll into an oval shape, cut half through the middle longways, pull cut abroad. Fill in with fresh meat (beef or pork) chopped and seasoned. Pinch edges of cut together; bake in a hot oven for 35 or 40 minutes.

St. Just W.I.

GINGERBREADS (1)

Ingredients:
    3 lbs. of flour   4 ozs. ginger (ground)
    1 lb. butter   2 ozs. carbonate of soda
    1 lb. brown sugar   4 ozs. mixed peel
    2 lbs. dark treacle   A little mixed spice

Method: The carbonate of soda is mixed with a little milk and added last. Well mix, divide into portions, roll out on a floured board by hand like long sausages, cut into small pieces, roll these in the hand into round balls about the size of walnuts, place on greased baking sheath, allowing room to spread. Bake in a hot oven about ten minutes. They must be watched carefully. When taken out of oven, slip off the baking tin by putting a knife underneath. Put on a dish to cool and pack in tins.

If kept airtight they keep a long time.

Falmouth W.I. Centre.

This recipe was given to a Falmouth member by a woman who made and sold them at a stall in the streets in Redruth.

GINGERBREADS (2)

Ingredients:
    1½ lbs. flour   5 ozs. butter
    ¾ lb. brown sugar   ½ cup milk
    1 oz. lemon peel   ¾ oz. ground ginger
    2 teaspoonsful carbonate of soda

Method: Mix with treacle and bake until brown through in a warm oven.

Portscatho W.I.

THINK TO-DAY SPEAK TOMORROW

CAKES, ETC.

FIGGIE HOBBIN

Take a little suet, a little lard, teaspoonful baking powder, rub this into ½ lb. flour, add figs* to taste. Mix with cold milk or water to a stiff paste. Roll into 4 inch squares about ¼ inch thick. Cut across the top and bake ½ hour.

PERRANPORTH W.I.

Sometimes called figgy duff. A notice was seen in a shop window not long since, "Figgy Duff, 4d. lb. More Figgier, 5d."

" CURRANY 'OBBIN "

Make a stiffish paste with flour and lard and a pinch of salt, not no baking powder. Wet it up with milk if you got it, and water if you ab'n got it. Roll it out nice and thin and sprinkle it all over with currans, nice and thick. Then roll it up careful like you would your starch clothes, squeeze home the ends and brish it over with the white of an egg if you want it to shine. Then clap 'en in the ob'n. The children do dearly like it, and as they say currans be full of they new fangled "vitamines" the Doctors be always ordering, they ought to be good for 'em.

P.S.—If you get tired of currans you can make a "figgy" wan fer a change.

P.P.S.—Figs is just Cornish for raisins.

ST. KEA W.I.

FIGGY 'OBEN

Roll out some light pastry, cover with figs and lemon peel; roll up like a Swiss roll and make a light pattern on the top. Bake in a moderate oven.

TRURO W.I. CENTRE.

GROVEY CAKE

After pig-killing, when the fat had been rendered down to lard, the dried "groves" remaining were made into a heavy cake with barley flour and salt to taste. This was cut into square pieces when hot, and eaten at once.

MULLION W.I.

---

* Figs—Raisins.

PITCHY CAKE

Take some dough of bread after it has risen and work in (i.e. "pitch" in) some goodness (fat), currants and sugar. Let it rise again for a short time and bake.

CALLESTICK.

POTATO CAKE (1)

Take equal parts of boiled mashed potatoes, flour, and fine grated suet. Sqeeze together lightly with fingers, roll into shape required, lightly cut criss-cross. Bake in hot oven or on a baking iron under a kettle.

ST. JUST W.I.

POTATO CAKE (2)

Mash cooked potatoes finely. Add, if necessary, a little milk. Add a little flour till it is firm enough to pat into a cake, and a pinch of salt. Cook on a griddle (biscuit-tin lid would do) on a clear fire. Do not turn till browned on one side. 10 minutes or even less.

POLKERRIS W.I.

POTATO CAKE (3)

Ingredients:
1 lb. flour
1 lb. boiled potatoes, cold
½ lb. grated suet
2 ozs. sugar
1 oz. peel
Pinch of salt
¼ lb. currants

Method: Mix all together with milk or butter-milk, into a stiff dough, roll out and put on baking sheath, lightly cut in squares with knife, and bake in hot oven.

ST. MAWGAN W.I.

POTATO CAKE (4)

Take 12 medium-sized potatoes, clean and boil in skins until soft, then peel and mash while hot. Have ready in basin 1 sifted cup of flour, 1 tablespoon of butter, put mashed potatoes in with the flour and butter and half a cup of milk until an ordinary-looking pastry is made. Roll out on flour-board and put in a baking dish. With side of hand make hollows in pastry. Have ready enough bacon rashers (or, if preferred, any sliced fresh meat) to put on

---

A BALD HEAD IS SOON SHAVED

CAKES, ETC. 21

top of potato cake in the hollows made by hand. Bake in moderate oven until light brown.

MANACCAN W.I.

This recipe won a prize in the Australian Women's Mirror June 25th, 1929, and was given to the prize winner by a native of Camborne who went to Australia in 1869.

POTATO CAKES

Take 1 lb. boiled potatoes, nice and floury. Any left over from dinner will do, and if slightly warm, so much the better. Mash them free from lumps with 1 oz. butter, and a little salt. Work in just enough flour to enable you to knead them into a workable dough. Plentifully flour board, rolling pin and hands, and roll out dough to quarter inch thickness. Cut into rounds with tumbler. Place these on floured oven sheet in hot oven, near bottom heat, when underside is brown, turn. They are cooked in a few minutes. Spread with butter and serve very hot.

TRURO W.I. CENTRE.

SAFFRON

This, as is well known, is as much a delicacy in Cornwall as the pasty. A small quantity goes a long way, as it is expensive. It is usually sold in drams or half-drams. At the moment it is fairly cheap, the present (April, 1929) price being 6s. 10d. per ounce. There is a well-known Cornish proverb, " As dear as Saffron."

It is a moot point when Saffron was first introduced into Cornwall. It is popularly believed the Phœnicians brought it over with them when they came to trade for tin. The following description of how to grow it was taken from an old book dated 1698.

Saffron is a great Improver of Land, and will grow in indifferent good Ground where it is not Stony nor too Wet, and in this case having Ploughed your Ground into Ridglands, as for Corn or Pease, take your Roots (a Bushel of which will set an Acre), and having drawn a Drill with a large Hoe, place them therein with the Spurns downwards, about three inches asunder; then draw another Drill, so that the mold of it may cover up the former, and in that place others in the same manner, and successively, till you have set your Roots, and when they Spring up, draw Earth about them, and these you must set in the beginning of July, and if the Weather be exceeding dry, you may sometimes water the top ranges, and in September the Blew Flower appears, and in it upon opening, three or four Blades of Saffron, which you must observe to gather out Morning and Evening for a Month together, the Flowers continually encreasing.

The Saffron being gathered, you must make a Kiln, about half the bigness of a Bee Hive, of Clay and Sticks, and so putting a gentle Fire of Charcoal under it, tend it by often turning, till you have reduced three pound of wet Saffron to one of dry; and in this case

---

OUT OF SIGHT OUT OF MIND

one Acre of Saffron will amount to the value of between Forty and Fifty pounds in Money, the two Crops, for the Roots will yield effectually no more, without being renewed or transplanted, and thus much for the improvement of Land, by these profitable means and methods.

The method of making these is similar in each recipe given. The ingredients vary, according to quality and quantity desired.

SAFFRON CAKE (1)

Ingredients:

4½ lbs. flour	1 oz. yeast
¾ lb. currants	Saffron
¾ lb. sultanas	¼ lb. lemon peel
1 lb. lard	½ lb. castor sugar
½ lb. butter	Pinch salt
4 eggs	Warm milk to mix

TRURO W.I. CENTRE.

SAFFRON CAKE (2)

Take a quartern of fine flour, a pound and a half of butter, three ounces of caraway seeds, six eggs well beaten, a quarter of an ounce of cloves and mace fine beaten together, a little pounded cinnamon, a pound of sugar, a little rose-water and saffron, a pint and a half of yeast, and a quart of milk. Mix all together lightly in the following manner:—First boil your milk and butter, then skim off the butter, and mix it with your flour, and a little of the milk. Stir the yeast into the rest, and strain it. Mix it with the flour, put in your seeds and spice, rose-water, tincture of saffron, sugar and eggs. Beat it all well up, and bake it in a hoop or pan well buttered. Send it to a quick oven, and an hour and a half will do it.

TRURO W.I. CENTRE.

This is an old recipe dated 1805.

SAFFRON CAKE (3)

4 lbs. flour, 1½ lbs. butter, 1¾ lbs. currants, 1½ lbs. sugar, 6 ozs. lemon peel, a dram saffron, a little grated nutmeg, 2 ozs. of yeast.

TINTAGEL W.I.

SAFFRON CAKE (4)

8¾ lbs. flour, ¼ lb. yeast, 6 ozs. sugar, 5 lbs. butter or lard. 6 lbs. fruit, salt, peel, saffron.

TRURO W.I. CENTRE.

COLD HANDS, WARM HEART

CAKES, ETC.

SAFFRON CAKE (5)

4 lbs. flour, 1½ lbs. of lard, ½ lemon peel, 1½ lbs. currants or sultanas, ¼ of salt, 2 ozs. yeast.

REDRUTH W.I. CENTRE.

SAFFRON CAKE (6)

Ingredients:
- 4½ lbs. flour
- 6 ozs. mixed peel
- 2 lbs. currants
- 1¾ lbs. butter and lard
- ⅛ oz. saffron
- ½ lb. sugar
- ½ nutmeg
- Milk, salt
- 2 ozs. yeast

Method: Well mix dry ingredients, then put in yeast, leave till light and bake 1¼ hours.

FALMOUTH W.I. CENTRE.

SAFFRON CAKE (7)

Ingredients:
- 4½ lbs. flour
- 2 lbs. currants
- 1 lb. butter
- 1 lb. lard
- ½ lb. brown sugar
- ½ lb. peel
- 2 ozs. yeast
- Saffron
- Nutmeg   To taste
- Salt

Bake 1¼ hours.

TRURO W.I. CENTRE.

SAFFRON CAKE (8)

Ingredients:
- 3 lbs. flour
- 1 lb. butter and lard
- 1 lb. currants
- ¼ lb. peel
- 1 drachm saffron
- ¼ lb. moist sugar
- A little nutmeg
- A teaspoonful salt

Bake 1½ hours.

TRURO W.I. CENTRE.

SAFFRON CAKE (9)

Ingredients:
- 6 lbs. flour
- 2 lbs. lard
- ½ lb. butter
- 3 lbs. currants
- 1 lb. moist sugar
- ½ lb. peel
- ½ nutmeg
- 6d. saffron
- 1 dessertspoonful salt
- 4 ozs. yeast

TRURO W.I. CENTRE.

ALL IS NOT GOLD THAT GLITTERS

SAFFRON CAKE (10)

For this take 2 lbs. flour, 1 lb. fat (lard, butter, or a mixture of these), ¼ lb. sugar, 2 ozs. mixed peel finely shredded, 1 lb. currants or sultanas (or mixed), 1 oz. yeast, warm milk, or milk and water.

Rub fat thoroughly into flour, add sugar and good pinch of salt. Put yeast in a cup with teaspoonful sugar, add little warm milk—not hot, but more than tepid.

When yeast rises in cup make a pit in flour and pour the yeast in with little more warm milk, turn a little flour over it. When this cracks and the yeast sponges through, mix into a soft dough with the hand, using milk as required. Add saffron when mixing. Add fruit, put a warm plate on it and stand it in a warm place until the mixture raises the plate and appears light and spongy.

Part may be made into buns or the whole baked in cake tins. In either case allow to " rise " for a short time before baking. Buns 15 to 20 minutes, cakes three-quarters or one hour, according to size.

To prepare saffron, take half drachm and cut very fine with scissors, pour over half cup boiling water and steep over night.

LOSTWITHIEL W.I.

SEED CAKE

Ingredients:
- ½ lb. flour
- 3 ozs. butter
- 1 dessertspoon caraway seeds
- 1 teaspoon baking powder
- 4 ozs. castor sugar
- 3 eggs

Method: Beat butter and sugar to a cream, beat yolks of eggs well and add with flour and baking powder, whisk whites to a stiff froth and mix lightly in, add caraway seeds, pour into a tin lined with greased paper, bake in moderate oven 1½ hours.

PORTSCATHO W.I.

SEEDY CAKE

Ingredients:
- 4 ozs. flour
- 4 ozs. sugar
- 4 ozs. butter
- 1 teaspoonful caraway seeds
- 2 eggs
- Pinch of salt

Method: Cream butter and sugar, whisk yolks and whites of eggs separately, add, gradually, flour, yolks and whites,

---

A BLACK PLUM IS AS SWEET AS A WHITE

CAKES, ETC.

also caraway seeds. Bake half hour to three-quarters hour in quick oven.

TRURO W.I. CENTRE.

SLY CAKES

Roll out some flaky pastry thin, cover half with currants and chopped peel to taste; fold over the remainder of pastry and lightly roll. Sprinkle top with sugar, then cut into various shapes and bake.

TRURO W.I. CENTRE.

PLAIN SULTANA CAKE

Ingredients:
- 6 lbs. flour
- 1½ lbs. lard, butter or margarine
- 1 lb. sultanas
- 2 tablespoonsful moist sugar
- 1 teaspoonful salt
- 2 ozs. yeast

Method: Mix salt and flour, rub fat in, add sultanas and sugar, and a little lemon peel (if liked). Previously set yeast to work, and work it in as in making saffron cake. When risen put in bread tins, let it rise again and bake.

SHORTLANESEND W.I.

This recipe has been specially asked for by several visitors to Cornwall.

CORNISH SQUAB CAKE

Make a good pasty crust, mash potatoes and season with salt and pepper. Spread them over the tops of the crust and lay strips of pickled pork over it and put in the oven to brown it. Some people mix cream with the potatoes.

PENZANCE.

CORNISH SANDWICHES

Ingredients:
2 spoonsful of damson, whortleberry or blackberry jam. 2 spoonsful of clotted cream. Eight or nine little scones, very fresh, but cold.

Method: Rub the jam through a sieve, split the scones and remove part of the soft inside. Spread a little jam on each half of the scone, and a teaspoonful of thick cream on the lower half of each, press each scone together. These are best prepared only a short time before they are to be eaten.

TRURO W.I. CENTRE.

WILFUL WASTE MAKES WOEFUL WANT

CREAM

CLOTTED CREAM

Use new milk and strain at once, as soon as milked, into shallow pans. Let it stand for 24 hours in winter and 12 hours in summer. Then put the pan on the stove, or, better still, into a steamer containing water, and let it slowly heat until the cream begins to show a raised ring round the edge. When sufficiently cooked place in a cool dairy and leave for 12 or 24 hours. Great care must be taken in moving the pans, so that the cream is not broken, both in putting on the fire and taking off. When required skim off the cream in layers into a glass dish for the table, taking care to have a good "crust" on the top. Clotted cream is best done over a stick fire.

CORNISH BURNT CREAM

Put a layer of baked custard in the bottom of a pie-dish, then a layer of clotted cream, then more layers of custard and cream, until the dish is full. Slice some citron very thin and put on top. Sprinkle with castor sugar and lightly brown.

ST. DAY W.I.

FRIED EGGS AND CLOTTED CREAM

Fry the eggs quite brown and serve with a lump of clotted cream on top of each.

ST. DAY W.I.

JUNKET

Set a quart of new milk, with ½ pint cream in it, in a glass dish, with spoonful of rennet; pour over it ½ pint of white wine, 2 ozs. of sugar, and half a nutmeg grated. Cover with plain whisked cream and garnish with apricot jam or jelly.

ST. JUST W.I.

Recipe dated 1824.

SUCK CREAM

Boil 1 pint raw cream, add the yolk of an egg well beaten, 2 or 3 spoonsful of white wine, sugar and lemon peel to taste. Stir over a gentle fire until it be as thick as cream. Leave until cold. Serve in glasses with long pieces of dry toast.

BOSCASTLE.

SAY WELL IS GOOD, BUT DO WELL IS BETTER

FISH DISHES

ROAST BREAM

Ingredients:
    1 nice size bream   A little suet
    A little parsley   A little salt
    A few bread crumbs

Method: Clean and scale the Bream, chop parsley and suet. Stuff Bream with suet, parsley and bread crumbs, put in baking dish, sprinkle with suet and salt. Bake in oven until a golden brown, dripping continually.

N.B.—This dish is exceedingly good with boiled potatoes.

MADRON W.I.

TO BOIL A CRAB

Have a large pan of boiling water and a handful of salt, and plunge the crab into it. Let it boil quickly for about 20 minutes. It is better to lay the crab on its feet while boiling.

ST. FEOCK W.I.

DIPPIE

Boil potatoes and pilchards in thin cream or dippie.

This dish is called "Dippie" and was very popular before cream was demanded by the factories.

PENZANCE.

FISH PIE

Take some rock mackerel, fillet, and place in pie-dish, sprinkle bread crumbs, then chopped suet and parsley. Repeat until the dish is full, then pour milk over, and bake. If preferred a pie crust may be put over the dish as for an ordinary pie and baked.

BOSCASTLE.

RED GURNET (COLD)

Put the fish (cleaned and washed) into cold water with a sliced carrot, 2 onions, and a bunch of thyme, bay and parsley. Boil gently for half an hour. Remove flesh and pile in a dish.

BETTER A SMALL FISH THAN AN EMPTY DISH

For the sauce—Work a piece of butter and some flour together over the fire. Add some strained liquor from the fish till thick. Add lemon juice and yolks of 2 eggs so that they do not curdle. Season with pepper and salt and pour all over the fish. This is best if prepared the day before use. The sauce should be very thick and smooth.

BODMIN.

LANCES (SAND EELS)

Pinch off head, wash and dry. Fry.

To cure—soak for 12 hours in strong brine, string with needle and twine in lots of 20 to 30. Dry in sun. When required broil or soak overnight in water and boil.

ST. JUST W.I.

LIMPETS

Carefully wash the sand off the limpets, put on the fire in a pan of cold water, and boil until they slip out of their shells. Serve cold with vinegar and pepper.

MULLION W.I.

TO ROAST LOBSTERS

Take ye Lobsters alive and as fresh as you can, wash them clean, lay them fast to ye Spitt and roast them three-quarters of an hour first—basting them with water and white wine vinegar seasoned very well with sweet herbs and onions, whole pepper and a good handful of salt, boil this, then baste ye Lobsters till a little before you draw them, then baste them with butter and salt and shake a little flower over them to make them froth, then draw them, split ye tails and crack ye claws and dish it, having sauce ready, viz., butter, anchovies, a little white wine, nutmeg and small pepper, a blade or two of whole mace, ye juice of a lemon or some vinegar, shake in some flower or crumbs of bread to thicken it, either serve with ye Lobster or in a plate by itself. Garnish with sliced lemon or any green parsley or Horse-radish.

PENZANCE.

Dated 1727.

HE WAS A BOLD MAN WHO FIRST ATE AN OYSTER

FISH DISHES

MARINATED MACKEREL

Ingredients:
- 4 or more mackerel
- 2 chopped bay leaves
- 6 cloves
- Blade of mace
- Sprig of thyme
- 1 onion
- 10 peppercorns
- Salt and vinegar

Method: Clean and prepare mackerel and arrange in a pie-dish, chop the onion and parsley and sprinkle over the fish. Add other ingredients with salt to taste. Pour over sufficient vinegar to cover well and bake in moderate oven for 40 or 50 minutes. When cooked put fish carefully on a dish and strain vinegar over them. Leave until cold and serve.

BOSCASTLE.

ROAST MACKEREL

Roast them with fennel; after they are roasted open them and take out the bone; then make a good sauce with butter, parsley and gooseberries, all seasoned; soak your mackerel a very little, with your sauce, then serve them hot.

1753. ST. STEPHENS W.I.

MULLET PIE

Cut fish in pieces, and stew in milk (one-third water). Add a good handful of parsley, and seasonings, put in pie-dish, and cover with crust in ordinary way. Time ½ to ¾ hour.

SENNEN W.I.

BROILED PILCHARDS

Gill them, wash them, dry them, season them with salt; then broil them over a gentle fire and baste them with butter; when they are enough, serve them up with beaten butter, mustard and pepper; or you may make a sauce of their own heads, squeezed between two trenchers, with some beer and salt.

1753. ST. STEPHENS W.I.

MARINATED PILCHARDS (1)

Clean pilchards, sprinkle with salt and pepper inside them (do not split quite open) and place a bay leaf in each one. Put them in a baking dish or earthenware pan, and nearly cover with equal quantities of vinegar and tea (cold),

MAKE NOT FISH OF ONE AND FLESH OF ANOTHER

a little brown sugar. Cover with brown paper and cook in slow oven until all bones are soft. Must be eaten cold.

GERRANS AND PORTSCATHO W.I.

MARINATED PILCHARDS (2)

Thoroughly clean and wash as many pilchards as will fill an earthenware jar or pan. Put a bay leaf inside each fish and season well with pepper and salt. When the pan is full of fish, pour in sufficient vinegar to cover them, tie down with brown paper and put into slow oven. Leave all night. It is usual to put this into an oven after the baking is finished, and if the bones of fish are dissolved by next morning, it is ready to serve. If not, return to oven until done. Must be eaten cold.

TRURO W.I. CENTRE.

SALTING PILCHARDS

Get a bussa (earthenware stain) or pan. Place the fish in layers, after cleaning, filling the insides with salt, and sprinkle salt thinly on each layer. Cover with a piece of old flannel. Put a stone on top.

PERRANPORTH W.I.

"SCROWLED" PILCHARDS

Clean fish and split quite open, mix teaspoonful salt, sugar and pepper, sprinkle well over them, and leave overnight. Then "scrowl" on gridiron over a clear fire.

GERRANS AND PORTSCATHO W.I.

TO PICKLE SPRATS

Take a Peck of the largest Sprats, without Heads, and Salt them a little over Night; then take a Pot or Barrell and lay in it a lay of Bay Salt; and then a lay of Sprats, and a few Bay Leaves with a little Lemon Peel, thus do till you have filled the Vessel, then cover and Pitch it that no Air get in, set it in a cool Cellar, and once a week turn it upside down; in three months you may eat them.

SHORTLANESEND.

This recipe it dated **1698**.

SOME ARE WISE, SOME ARE OTHERWISE

A TROUT PYE

Clean, wash and scale them, lard them with Pieces of a Silver Eel rolled up in Spice and sweet Herbs, and Bay Leaves powder'd; lay on and between them the bottoms of slic'd Artichokes, Mushrooms, Oysters, Capers and slic'd Lemon; lay on Butter, and close the Pye.

TRURO.

Dated 1738.

PASTIES

THE CORNISH PASTY

The Cornish pasty is, and has been from time immemorial, the staple dish of the County, and in giving various Recipes for making it, it may be noted that the method does not vary, but the name of the pasty varies according to the filling, or inside.

Therefore the general method of making has been given, and a list of various kinds of pasties afterwards.

It is said that the Devil has never crossed the Tamar into Cornwall, on account of the well-known habit of Cornishwomen of putting everything into a pasty, and that he was not sufficiently courageous to risk such a fate! However, that may be, the Cornish pasty, in its various forms, is a delectable dainty and deservedly world-famous.

When the pasties are being made, each member of the family has his or hers marked at one corner with the initial of the prospective owner. In this way each person's tastes can be catered for.

The true Cornish way to eat a pasty is to hold it in the hand, and begin to bite it from the opposite end to the initial, so that, should any of it be uneaten, it may be consumed later by its rightful owner. And woe betide anyone who takes another person's " corner! "

A CORNISH PASTY

Pastry rolled out like a plate,
  Piled with " turmut, tates, and mate."
Doubled up, and baked like fate,
  That's a " Cornish Pasty."—(Original.)

BREAGE.

PASTY

Any good pastry may be used but it should not be too flaky nor too rich. A very useful pastry is:

1 lb. flour, ½ lb. lard and suet, ½ teaspoonful salt, mix with water.

EVERYONE TO HIS TASTE

When pastry is made, roll out about ¼ inch thick, and cut into rounds with a plate to the size desired.

Lay the rounds on the pastry board with half of the round over the rolling pin and put in the fillings, damp the edges lightly and fold over into semi-circle. Shape the pasty nicely and "crimp" the extreme edges where it is joined between the finger and thumb. Cut a slit in the centre of the pasty, lay on a baking sheet and bake in a quick oven, so that it keeps its shape.

APPLE PASTY

Peel apples, slice thinly, and lightly sprinkle with brown sugar. In Summer-time blackberries are usually mixed with the apple.

BROCCOLI PASTY

Boil broccoli until nearly cooked, but still quite firm, strain it, and fill pasty in usual way, adding salt.

LAMBOURNE W.I.

CHICKEN PASTY

Chicken cut up in small pieces.

DATE PASTY

Stone dates and fill in the usual way.

EGGY PASTY

Bacon cut in dice, parsley and one or two eggs, according to size of pasty required.

HERBY PASTY

Prepare pastry as for ordinary pasty. Well wash equal quantities of parsley, bits,* shallots (early), half quantity spinach, prepare some slices of bacon cut into small pieces and an egg well beaten. Pour boiling water over the parsley, bits, and spinach that have been cut into small portions, and let stand for half an hour, well squeeze all moisture out. Put on pastry with the shallots cut finely and the bacon, pinch up the edges of pasty allowing a small portion left open for the egg to be added, finish pinching and bake.

BOSCASTLE.

---

* Bits is a common herb believed to be found only in N. Cornwall. It is found in the hedges and on the cliffs. Gypsies pick it for medicinal purposes.

PASTIES

JAM PASTY
These are usually made smaller than a savoury pasty, and any kind of jam may be used.

MACKEREL PASTY
Allow one or two mackerel to each pasty, and clean and boil them in usual way. Then remove skin and bones, and lay on pastry; fill up with washed parsley, and add pepper and salt. Finish as above.

MEAT AND POTATO PASTY
Always use fresh steak, potatoes cut small, salt and pepper, flavoured with onion.

PARSLEY PASTY
Parsley and lamb or mutton.

PORK PASTY
Fresh pork, and potatoes, flavoured with onion, sage or thyme.

RABBITTY PASTY
Use fleshy part of rabbit cut us the same as meat, fairly small.

RICE PASTY
Cook some rice in milke as if for pudding, sweeten and mix with an egg; make some good short pastry, fill with the cooked rice and bake in a good sized pasty until pastry is well done.

Shortlanesend W.I.

SOUR SAUCE PASTY
Gather a quantity of sour sauce (sorrel) leaves. Shrink them by pouring boiling water and use the leaves in a pasty. Serve with sugar and cream.

Mullion W.I.

STAR-GAZING PASTY
Mawther used to get a herring, clean 'un, and put same stuffin' as what yow do have in mabiers (chicken); sew 'en up with niddle and cotton, put 'en in some daugh made of suet and flour; pinch the daugh up in the middle and lave the heid sticking out one end, and tail t'other. They was some nice pasties, too, cooked in a fringle fire with crock and brandis and old furzy tobs.

E. R.

DO NOT PUT ALL YOUR EGGS IN ONE BASKET

TURNIP PASTY

Turnips and potatoes, sometimes all turnip with a lump of butter or cream. Or fat bacon may be used.

WINDY PASTY

Take the last bit of pastry left over from making pasties, roll it into a round, fold over and crimp as for ordinary pasty. Bake in oven and when done (whilst still hot) open out flat and fill each side with jam. It may be eaten hot or cold.

GWENNAP.

PIES

APPLE AND SPICE PIE

Roll out some pastry the size of a dinner-plate and put on a greased plate. Cut up 1 lb. apples, add 2 ozs. sugar, ½ lb. currants, 1 heaped teaspoon of ground mixed spice, and some finely-chopped lemon peel. Roll out another piece of pastry the size of a dessert plate, place on mixture, press the edges of the two pieces of pastry together and crimp them with a fork. Bake in a moderate oven.

TRURO W.I. CENTRE.

APPLE AND MUTTON PIE

Make in same way as Apple and Spice Pie, adding ¼ lb. chopped mutton and 1 finely chopped small onion.

TRURO W.I. CENTRE.

AN EEL PYE

Cut, wash, and season them with sweet seasoning, a handful of currants, butter, and close it.

TRURO.

This is dated 1738.

CONGER PIE (1)

Cut fish in fairly small steaks (the middle fish is best part), put into a pie-dish, add chopped parsley, pepper and salt, and three-quarter fill the dish with milk and water. Partly cook pie before putting on the pastry, then put on the crust and finish in a fairly hot oven. Five minutes before serving, lift the pastry and add a little cream.

POLPERRO W.I.

HE THAT WOULD THRIVE MUST RISE AT FIVE

PIES

CONGER PIE (2)
From slices of Conger break off pieces about the size of an egg, roll in a mixture of pepper, salt and flour. Between layers of fish place chopped parsley, a little butter, and egg. When fish reaches top of dish, pour in milk to half fill the dish. Sprinkle bread crumbs on top and bake.

St. Just W.I.

CURLEW PIE
Pluck and clean curlews, fill the bodies with onions, put in pie-dish, cover with good pastry and bake until cooked.

Penzance.

DUCK PYE
Make a puff paste crust, take a couple of ducks, scald them, and make them very clean, cut off the feet, the pinions, the neck and head, all clean picked and scalded, with the gizzards, livers and hearts; pick out all the fat of the insides, lay a crust all over the dish, season the ducks with pepper and salt, inside and out, lay them in your dish, and the giblets at each end seasoned; put in as much water as will almost fill the pye, lay on the crust, and bake it, but not too much.

St. Stephens W.I.

1753.

GIBLET PIE
Clean two pairs of giblets well, and put all but the livers into a saucepan, with two quarts of water, twenty corns of whole pepper, three blades of mace, a bundle of sweet herbs, and a large onion. Cover them close, and let them stew very gently till they are tender. Have a good crust ready. Cover your dish, lay at the bottom a fine rump steak seasoned with pepper and salt, put in your giblets, with the livers, and strain the liquor they were stewed in; then season it with salt, and pour it into your pie. Put on the lid, and bake it an hour and a half.

Lambourne W.I.

Dated 1805.

GOOSE GIBLET PIE
Ingredients:
　　1 or 2 sets goose giblets, apples, spice, currants, raisins, moist sugar and nutmeg.

Method: Prepare and clean all ingredients, put together in a large pie-dish, cover with pastry and bake well in a good oven.

Tintagel W.I.

FAIR WORDS BUTTER NO PARSNIPS

HERBY PIE (1)

Take two handsful of parsley leaves, one of spinach, mustard cress, white beet leaves, and one handful of finely sliced lettuce hearts, three or four borage leaves and a dozen chives. Wash these herbs well, and boil them for three or four minutes. Drain the water from them, chop them small, season with salt and pepper and spread them in a buttered dish. Make a batter with five tablespoonsful of flour and a pinch of salt, mixed smoothly with two eggs and as much milk as will bring it to the consistence of thick cream. Pour this over the herbs, stir all well together and bake in a moderate oven. If liked the edges of the dish can be lined with good pastry.

St. Agnes W.I.

HERBY PIE (2)

Line a pie-dish with bacon. Take parsley, water-cress or pepper-cress, leeks, shallots (or small quantity sweet leeks) and spinach. Scald and chop these herbs and mix all together. Beat an egg or two. Fill dish and put one or two layers more of streaked bacon, pour the beaten eggs over all, add a little water or stock. Put on thin pastry crust, and bake according to size and thickness, say 1½ hours.

St. Newlyn East W.I.

Some people put blackcurrant leaves, potato tops, wild orange.

HERBY PIE (3)

Line a pie-dish with bacon, chop small and parboil or scald parsley, water-cress or pepper-cress, leeks or shallots, or sweet leek (small quantity), spinach.

(Some put blackcurrant leaves, potato tops, wild orange). All mixed together. Beat an egg or two. Fill dish, put one or two layers more of streaked bacon, pour beaten eggs over all, add a little water or stock. Put on thin pastry crust and bake according to size and thickness, say 1½ hours.

From Old Members of St. Newlyn East W.I.

LAN'CEN (LAUNCESTON) PIE

Pieces of meat placed at the bottom of a pie-dish, seasoned with pepper and salt, then sliced potatoes to nearly fill the dish, more seasoning, and little water. Add

---

SOME MEN ARE BORN TO FEAST AND NOT TO FIGHT

PIES

a few small whole potatoes on the top and a roll of pastry as a ring of crust round the edge of the dish. Bake under a kettle in the open chimney.

> The round "hearth" was set on a heap of hot ashes, the pie put on it, and a baking "kettle" turned over it; then a ring of ashes where the "hearth" and "kettle" met, to keep out the smoke. Then furze was piled on and fired until thought to be enough, when a heap of "bruss" (the dust of the furze rick) was heaped on to smoulder and retain the heat.
>
> I have often seen the cook put the fire-hook (for handling the furze) on the edge of the "hearth" and bend to listen if the pie was boiling. This mode of listening for sounds was common.
>
> I have heard an old man telling how, in his boyhood, they listened with the hook on the hearthstone in the days when Napoleon was a terror, and his landing on the coast dreaded at every cove, fearing to hear the tramp of his soldiers and the rolling of their drums.

LEEK PIE

Wash, clean and chop about half-dozen good-sized leeks, put in a pan and cover with boiling water, drain in colander; put a layer in a pie-dish, then some fat bacon very finely sliced; then another layer of leek and bacon until dish is filled. Salt to taste, sufficient milk to cover; boil for half an hour on top of stove, then cover with good suet pastry; ten minutes before ready for the table, beat up two eggs and a spoonful of cream, remove the pastry and lay beaten eggs, etc., over the cooked leeks, replace pastry and put back in the oven for ten minutes.

Shortlanesend W.I.

"LIKKY" PIE

Ingredients:
- 12 leeks
- ½ lb. green bacon
- ¼ lb. cream
- 2 eggs
- Some milk for gravy

Method: Take the leeks and cut in small pieces, scald about ten minutes in boiling water. Cut bacon in very thin slices. Put a layer of bacon in the bottom of pie-dish, then a layer of leeks, and continue each layer until dish is full, season with pepper and salt. Cover with suet crust. Have ready ¼ lb. cream, two well-beaten eggs, beaten separately (whites and yolks). When pie is cooked, take off crust and drain off all liquid from the pie and substitute the cream and eggs.

Truro W.I. Centre.

WASTE NOT, WANT NOT

LEEK AND POTATO PIE

Use 1 lb. shin beef, 3 leeks, and potatoes, as many as required.

Method: Cut the beef in rather small pieces and stew gently one hour in the pie-dish with the potatoes cut in quarters. Wash and clean leeks, drain them, and put on top of dish. Make a pastry with 2 ozs. chopped suet and a little lard mixed with flour; cover the dish and bake until nice and brown.

FLUSHING W.I.

MINCE PIES (1)

Ingredients:

1 lb. sultanas
1 lb. currants
1 lb. figs (raisins)
½ lb. best beef suet
1 lb. demerara sugar

½ lb. mixed peel
4 ozs. blanched sweet almonds
Allspice to taste
2 lbs. peeled and chopped apples

Method: Mix all these together, then put through a mincing machine. Add a wineglassful of rum or brandy. Tie up and store in a cool place till needed.

TRURO W.I. CENTRE.

The Cornish Christmas Mince Pie used to be made oblong in shape, in imitation of the manger where our Saviour was laid.

MINCE PIES (2)

Ingredients:

3 lbs. chopped suet (beef)
3 lbs. chopped apples
3 lbs. figs (raisins)
4 lbs. currants
1 lb. sultanas
1½ lbs. moist sugar

2 lbs. mixed peel and citron
2 nutmegs, grated
1 oz. salt
½ oz. ground ginger
½ oz. ground coriander seeds
½ oz. allspice
¼ oz. cloves

Grated rinds of 6 lemons and 6 oranges, juice of same. Sherry or brandy to moisten.

TRURO W.I. CENTRE.

MUGGETY PIE (1)

Prepare a sheep's pluck by soaking in water and thoroughly cleaning. Boil for several hours, and when cooked put through mincing machine; then add a few currants, season well, and flavour with parsley or spice. Mix well together, put into a pie-dish, cover with a good short crust, and bake three-quarters hour.

CALLINGTON W.I.

DO NOT BUY A PIG IN A POKE

MUGGETY PIE (2)

Take the long cord of a calf, clean it, soak for an hour in salt water and then boil a short time. Cut cord lengthways with a pair of scissors. Cut into convenient lengths, place in pie-dish with pepper, salt, and flour to taste. Add onions, if liked, and a white sauce. Cover with pastry and bake.

St. Just W.I.

This is regularly sold at the present day in Penzance on market days.

MUGGETY PIE (3)

Take the pots* of a pig, wash them and place in a pie-dish with plenty of onions, pepper and salt. Cover with pastry and bake.

Pendeen W.I.

PARSLEY PIE (1)

Boil a quantity of parsley until tender. Chop it finely and almost fill a pie-dish. Add some pieces of lamb, mutton or veal, and hard-boiled eggs, also some very good stock. Season well, and bake with a short crust. When done raise the crust carefully and stir 3 tablespoonsful of cream.

Bodmin.

PARSLEY PIE (2)

Line a deep, round tin with good short crust. Wash about three handsful fresh parsley thoroughly and lay half of it in bottom of the tin; cut two rashers of smoked bacon into small pieces, and lay on parsley. Break on this three or four fresh eggs, distributing them evenly. Season well with pepper and salt, and lay remainder of parsley on top. Cover the top with a thin crust, make a hole in centre, and bake till well browned in hot oven.

Lostwithiel W.I.

ROOK PIE

Skin the rooks and cut up, using only the breasts and legs, and soak overnight in slightly salted milk and water. Lay strips of bacon along the sides and bottom of a pie-dish, fill up the dish with layers of rooks and bacon strips, seasoned with salt and pepper. Add 2 ozs. cream and milk to cover. Cover top with short or puff pastry and bake about 1½ hours.

---

* Pots are the intestines of a pig.

STAR-GAZING PIE

Ingredients:
Required, pastry, fish (6 or more pilchards preferably), pepper and salt, 2 or 3 hard-boiled eggs, if liked.

Method: Prepare pastry, put the pilchards in pie-dish whole, and with heads left on, well season with pepper and salt, add eggs, cut in slices, lay pastry over and put the mouths of the pilchards through the pastry so that they can be seen (hence the name).

BOSCASTLE.

STAR-GAZY PIE (1)

Take as many fresh herrings or mackerel as will fill a moderate sized dish. Scale, and open them, and remove the bones. Lay them flat on the table, season the inside of each with salt, pepper and chopped parsley, and roll it up neatly. Butter the pie-dish and sprinkle upon it a thick layer of finely grated bread crumbs. Lay in some of the fish and fill the dish with alternate layers of fish and bread crumbs. Cover the contents with a few slices of fat bacon pour over all six eggs beaten up with two tablespoonsful of tarragon vinegar, or, if preferred, a quarter of a pint of cream. Cover the dish with a good crust and bake in a well heated oven. Arrange the heads of the fish in the centre of the pastry; when the pie is baked put a piece of parsley into the mouth of each fish and serve.

ST. AGNES W.I.

STAR-GAZY PIE (2)

Clean and scale 7 or 8 pilchards, remove heads, pepper and salt inside of fish. Place in a pie-dish, or better as for pie cake, viz., roll out pastry in two rounds, place fish on larger, cover with smaller, cut slits and insert heads of pilchards gazing up. When a pie-dish is used potato crust is usually used.

ST. JUST W.I.

SQUAB PIE (1)

Use young squabs,* onions, apples, a little mutton. Clean squabs, and fill a pie-dish with them and above ingredients. Put on good pastry and bake in hot oven.

BODMIN.

* Squabs are young pigeons. Sometimes young cormorants were used, but they had to be skinned before being used.

SOME WOMEN ARE ALWAYS TRYING; OTHERS VERY

SQUAB PIE (2)

Peel and slice some apples into the bottom of a pie-dish. Next a layer of sliced onions, then slices of fat mutton, and a little salt. Then another layer of onions, slices apple on the top and a sprinkling of cooking sugar; cover with a crust and bake.

GRAMPOUND W.I.

SQUAB PIE (3)

Use giblets of duck (neck, liver, gizzard, wings, feet, and any other meatless parts). Cook these till tender, put in a pie-dish with chopped onions, apples, and a sprinkling of currants; season to taste, cover with pastry and bake in a moderate oven until onions and apples are cooked.

KILKHAMPTON W.I.

SQUAB PIE (4)

Place a layer of finely-sliced apples on the bottom of a deep pie-dish, then a layer of beef cut into small pieces. Chop a medium-sized onion fine and lay on the beef, with a sprinkling of ground spice, and then a layer of moist sugar. Then repeat the layers until the dish is full, and add a little water to prevent burning; cover with pastry and bake $2\frac{1}{2}$ hours if the dish is fairly large.

MANACCAN W.I.

SQUAB PIE (5)

As taught by the Phœnicians when they mined tin in Cornwall.

Ingredients according to size of pie. Mutton chops, all fat removed, bones boiled separately for stock.

Ingredients:

Apples, chopped fine	Sugar (brown sprinkled thinly)
Onions, chopped fine	
Currants	Spice, very little, also salt
	Stock

Method: Pie-dish, brown earthenware preferred. Put layers of mutton, about three inches square, over bottom of pie-dish. Put layers of apples one inch thick, sprinkle sugar. Put layer of onions half-inch (only one layer onions), salt. Put layer currants half-inch, sprinkle spice

---

LAZY FOLKS TAKE THE MOST PAINS

or layer of apples. Then put layer of mutton as at first. Finish with layer of apples. Pour on small quantity of stock. Boil uncovered (except a dish on top) 1½ hours on slow fire. Make light, thin pastry, put on, and bake one hour in oven.

FROM OLD MEMBERS OF ST. NEWLYN EAST W.I.

SQUAB PIE (6)

Take ½ lb. veal and cut into small square pieces and put a layer of them in the bottom of a large pie-dish. Sprinkle over these a portion of herbs, spices, seasoning, lemon peel and the yolks of eggs cut in slices. Cut ½ lb. of boiled ham very thin, and put in a layer of this. Take ½ lb. mutton, cut in pieces, and put in a layer of this, sprinkle as before with herbs and spices. Take ½ lb. beef cut in nice pieces and put a layer of these on top of the mutton, sprinkle as before with herbs and spices. Clean and skin a cormorant, cut up and put a layer on top of the beef and sprinkle as before with herbs and spices. Cut up half a dozen apples very thin, also half a dozen onions; mix and proceed to ram apples and onions into every conceivable crevice.

Take half a dozen pilchards, remove the bone and chop up, and strew the whole pie with pilchards. Then fill up with clotted cream until the pie can hold no more. Cover with crust, or ornament with leaves, brush over with yolk of an egg, and bake in a well-heated oven for 1 or 1¼ hours, or longer should the pie be very large or the cormorant very tough.

PENZANCE.

SQUAB PIE (7)

Ingredients:
    ½ lb. mutton
    1 lb. apples
    ¼ lb. sultanas or currants or figs

    Sugar to taste
    Mixed spice to taste
    Onion, if liked, a little
    Seasoning, salt and pepper

Method: Cut up the meat and apples. Mix in the other ingredients and season. Place in pie-dish with a little water and cover with paste. Bake in oven.

POLKERRIS W.I.

EAT TO LIVE, NOT LIVE TO EAT

PUDDINGS

CHOP POTATO PUDDING

Ingredients:
    4 large potatoes   ¼ lb. suet
    2 tablespoonful of flour

Chop altogether on board, mix with a little water. Put in basin and either boil or steam for two hours.

TRURO W.I.

GERTY MEAT PUDDINGS

Thoroughly cleanse the inside of a pig with salt and allow it to soak overnight in brine. Take the lights, melt, heart and kidneys, cover with cold water and boil till cooked (¾ hour). Cast down fat and lard, mince scallops and the cooked heart, etc. Save the liquid the heart, etc., was boiled in and to every 3 quarts of liquid allow 1 quart groats, and boil till cooked. Add groats to minced ingredients and season with salt and pepper. Fill the skins with this mixture and boil gently ¾ hour.

Pig's blood added to the mixture before putting into the skins makes the above in "BLACK POTS."

ST. MELLION W.I.

GRANDMOTHER'S BIRTHDAY PUDDING

Ingredients:
    1 lb. flour   3 ozs. chopped mixed peel
    Good pinch salt   6 ozs. sultanas
    Grating of nutmeg   6 ozs. currants
    6 ozs. chopped suet

Method: Mix all well together and make into a stiff paste with milk. Place into a scalded and floured cloth, and tie loosely, plunge in boiling water and boil to a gallop for three hours. When dished up cut a piece out of top as large as a teacup, place inside 4 ozs. of coarse brown sugar, one tea cup of Cornish cream. Put in oven for two minutes and serve piping hot. There will be no left-overs.

KILKHAMPTON W.I.

THE PROOF OF THE PUDDING IS IN THE EATING

HELSTON PUDDING

Ingredients:
2 ozs. each of raisins, currants, suet, sugar, breadcrumbs and ground rice
Small piece candied peel
½ teaspoonful bi-carbonate soda
½ teaspoonful mixed spice
2 ozs. flour
Little salt and milk

Method: Clean fruit and cut peel finely. Dissolve soda in milk, mix together all dry ingredients and add milk. Pour all into a well-greased basin, cover with greased paper and a floured pudding cloth, stand in a saucepan of boiling water and boil for two hours.

BOSCASTLE.

HOGS PUDDING

Clean some pig skins, and let them soak in salt and water. Take fresh pork, lean and fat, put through the mincing machine, then add bread crumbs, thyme, salt, and pepper. Mix all well together, take skins out of water, dry, and stuff with the mixture tightly, then tie each end. Boil until cooked. To be eaten cold, or fried in slices, if preferred.

POTATO PUDDING

Take 1lb. boiled potatoes rubbed through a sieve, 4 ozs. fresh butter melted in ½ pt. of cream, 6 ozs. sugar, 6 eggs, 1 oz. currants, peel of one lemon, ½ a nutmeg grated, a teaspoonful of brandy; mix all together and either bake in a dish lined with pastry or steam in a mould.

ST. JUST W.I.
A.D. 1824.

PUDDEN SKINS

Some brave, big slices of taties, turmuts, and onions all mixed together with pepper and salt, and put in a pie-dish with a tidy piece of flesh (slightly salted pork) from Mawther's bussa.

Put 'en over to cooky, and have some skins (same as they do have for hogs' puddens) and mix flour, suet, oatmeal, and "figs" (i.e., raisins) (old Cornish) and an egg, mix 'en like a batter, lookey see! and shove batter in the skins, twist 'en round the flesh and cook light brown.

Same to we down-a-long as Haggis is to they up-a-long.

E. R.

EVERYTHING HATH AN END BUT A PUDDING HATH TWO

WHEAT-STACK PUDDING

Baked fig pudding (figgy) was the correct sweet on the "Great Day," as the main day of carrying in the big stack was called. At dinner it usually followed boiled ham or beef with vegetables.

MULLION W.I.

BEVERAGES

HERBY BEER

Pick a large handful of young stinging nettles, yarrow and wild sage. Take 2 gallons of water, add herbs, boil all together, then add 1½ lbs. sugar. When nearly cold add 2 ozs. yeast, and let it all stand till the next day. Then strain through a muslin, bottle and cork. Tie down corks firmly. It must not be drunk until three days old.

ST. ERME W.I.

HOT BEER

Made hot by pouring into a cone-shaped tin vessel and putting on the fire point down.

J. C. H.

NETTLE BEER

The best time to make this is early in the Spring when nettles are young and tender and plentiful, but you can keep on making it all summer if you like, and most likely you will, once you have tasted it. First put a glove on your left hand—unless you are one of those hard-handed people who are not afraid of nettles or anythings else—(a thick pair of stockings or high boots also are advisable). Then with shears and a basket or "frail" you sally forth. You cut off the tops only of young nettles, gather enough to fill your saucepan, whatever size it is. Wash the nettles and pack into the saucepan, cover with water, and let boil till liquid is a clear green, or at least one hour. Pour off in vessel containing white sugar—allowing 1 lb. to each quart of liquid—a little experimenting will soon give you the exact quantity to suit individual tastes. Stir till dissolved. When cooled to blood heat add small quantity of yeast. Set it in a warm or cool place according to the weather and the time of year, and next morning it will be ready to be strained and bottled. It makes a most delicious drink as well as a valuable spring medicine and tonic.

ST. KEA W.I.

THEY NEVER TASTE WHO ALWAYS DRINK

POKER BEER

By thrusting a red-hot poker in a pint of beer.

J. C. H.

RARE OLD BLACKBERRY DRINK

3 lbs. blackberries, 1 pint vinegar, put together and allow to soak 24 hours, strain and add 1 lb. of sugar and to every pint of juice add 6 cloves and 1 oz. of root ginger; boil together half an hour. Strain, then bottle; can be used any time after bottling.

BOSCASTLE W.I.

BLACKBERRY SYRUP

Ingredients:
- 12 lbs. blackberries
- 2 quarts water
- 5 ozs. tartaric acid
- $1\frac{1}{2}$ lbs. white sugar to each pint of fruit

Method: Let it stand 24 or 48 hours, then bottle. A little syrup added to a tumbler of water makes a most refreshing summer drink. It can be mixed with hot water in the winter. The syrup will keep good for years.

DEVORAN W.I.

A summer beverage.

BLACKBERRY VINEGAR (1)

Ingredients:
- 1 qt. of blackberries
- 1 pt. of vinegar

Method: Mash blackberries, pour vinegar over and let it stand in a bowl closely covered for 24 hours, strain through a flannel bag and to each pint of liquor add $\frac{3}{4}$ lb. of sugar, and boil 20 minutes or until it thickens; when cold, bottle.

Very good for colds, sore throats, and cold on the chest. Taken in a glass of hot water, one or two tablespoons, or you make it as strong as you like.

ST. AGNES W.I.

BLACKBERRY VINEGAR (2)

Put a quantity of blackberries into a jug or stew-jar. Fill up the jug with vinegar allowing a pint of vinegar to $1\frac{1}{2}$ lbs. blackberries. Let it stand 3 days in a warm place, then strain. Add one pound loaf sugar to each pint of juice. Boil for about 20 minutes, skim off top while boiling to get it clear. Bottle when cold. It looks like port wine. Two tablespoons added to a tumbler of hot water will relieve colds and sore throats.

FLUSHING W.I.

PURE WATER IS BETTER THAN BAD WINE

BLACKBERRY WINE

Put alternate layers of blackberries and white sugar in a jar until filled, let it stand until the jar is full of wine, then strain and put into bottles, adding to each 3 teaspoonsful of white sugar; cork bottles down tightly the same day.

LAMBOURNE W.I.

GRANNY'S BLACKBERRY WINE

Ingredients:
- 12 qts. of ripe blackberries
- 12 qts. of water
- 3 spoonsful of yeast
- 12 lbs. brown sugar
- 6 lbs. malaga raisins
- 1 oz. isinglass

Method: Crush blackberries with your hands in a kneading bowl, add water and yeast, and allow it to work three days, stirring five or six times a day. Strain thrugh a hair sieve and add sugar, stirring till dissolved. Then pour into cask. Stone and cut raisins and drop into cask. Dissolve isinglass in a little cider and pour into cask. Close up and allow to stand six months before bottling. This improves with keeping.

SUMMERCOURT W.I.

CIDER MEAT

Cut up some pieces of bread, as for soup, and put in a basin. Pour a little cider on the bread, and a little sugar, then a large cupful of boiling water.

I have known cider-meat, taken by persons suffering from bronchial complaints, to give them immediate relief.

MULLION W.I.

CORNISH PUNCH

Ingredients:
- 1 bottle Jamaica rum
- ½ bottle brown cognac
- 1 tumbler lemon juice
- A little of the rind
- 2—4 lbs. sugar to taste
- A little Benedictine

Method: Put in sugar, pour in lemon juice, rind. Then put in brandy and rum, the whole being in a gallon jug, fill up with boiling water poured from a height.

LAMBOURNE W.I.

This is a very old recipe and was used at Levant Mine for many generations.

A SLOW DRINK IS BETTER THAN A DRY SERMON

COWSLIP WINE (1)

Ingredients:
- 2 qts. of flowers to each gallon of water (measure flowers when freshly gathered and allow to dry)
- 3 lbs. of sugar to each gallon of water
- 1 teacupful of raisins to four gallons of liquor
- 3 Seville oranges
- 2 lemons (cut up)

Method: Pour boiling water on dried flowers. Let them stand three days, stirring three times each day. Strain the liquor, add the sugar, and boil for half an hour. When cold add yeast on a slice of toast and let it ferment. Next day, remove yeast, and strain liquor into cask; add raisins, oranges and lemons. Stand three months, then bottle it.

SUMMERCOURT W.I.

This is excellent for pulmonary ailments.

COWSLIP WINE (2)

Take 50 lbs. sugar, add 24 gallons of water. Boil it one hour, carefully skimming. Pour in tub; when cold add 12 pecks bruised cowslip flowers, with peel and juice of 20 lemons, and two quarterns of good ale yeast. Stir well for three days, then rack it into a clean cask, cowslips and all, with half a gallon of brandy. When it has done working, bung it close.

ST. NEWLYN EAST W.I.

From a very old book.

COWSLIP WINE (3)

To every gallon of water, weigh three pounds of lump sugar; boil the quantity half an hour, taking off the scum as it rises. When cool enough put into it a crust of toasted bread dipped in thick yeast; let the liquor ferment in the tub thrity-six hours, then into the cask put, for every gallon, the peel of two and rind of one lemon, and both of one Seville orange, and one gallon of cowslip pips; then pour on them the liquor. It must be carefully stirred every day for a week, then to every five gallons put in a bottle of brandy. Let the cask be close stopped and stand only six weeks before you bottle off. Observe to use the best corks.

PENPONDS W.I.

GOOD WINE NEEDS NO BUSH

BEVERAGES

COWSLIP WINE (4)

To every gallon of water allow 3 lbs. loaf sugar, the rind of an orange and a lemon, and the strained juice of a lemon. Boil the sugar and water together for half an hour, skim it carefully, then pour it over the rind and juice. Let is stand until new-milk warm, add four quarts cowslip pips or flowers, and to every six quarts of liquid put three large tablespoonsful of fresh yeast spread on toast. On the next day put the wine into a cask, which must be closely stopped. It will be fit to bottle or drink from the cask in seven weeks. Allow twenty-four or forty-eight hours to ferment. It must remain in the cask for seven weeks.

St. Agnes W.I.

DANDELION AND COWSLIP WINE

Ingredients:
- 1 gallon of freshly gathered flowers (half and half)
- 1 gallon water
- Rind of ½ lemon to every gallon liquor
- 1 tablespoonful yeast

Method: Pour boiling water on flowers and lemon peel. Let it stand a fortnight. Strain off liquor, add sugar and yeast, and let it ferment. Bottle and keep filling up with water while working. Cork tightly, and keep in a cool place.

Summercourt W.I.

EGG FLIP (1)

This should be made with white ale if it can be procured. Make one pint of ale warm, but not too hot. Beat up two or three eggs with 3 ozs. sugar and throw the eggs into the jug containing ale, and then throw both back into an empty warmed jug. This must be repeated quickly five or six times until all is well mixed together; then grate ginger and nutmeg over the top and the flip is quite ready. Serve in glasses while hot.

St. Agnes W.I.

EGG FLIP (2)

In some parts of Cornwall called Egg Flosh. Lightly beat (or flosh) an egg in a tumbler, add very hot milk, keeping the egg floshing. Sugar to taste and, if liked, a little grating of nutmeg.

J. C. H.

OLD FRIENDS AND OLD WINE ARE BEST

EGG FLIP OR SAMPSON

Drink for a cold. Heat 1 quart cider in a large saucepan. Beat two eggs with 2 tablespoonsful sugar in a large jug. When the cider is hot pour a portion on to the beaten eggs and then back to the pan again, until the whole is a frothy mixture.

TREVELLAS W.I.

EGGY FLIP

Beat up an egg with a teaspoonful of sugar, grate a little nutmeg on it, and add a breakfast cupful of hot milk—not boiling.

TRURO W.I. CENTRE.

EGGIOT
(Pronunciation on the last syllable " ot.")

Beat up an egg in a tumbler, add one teaspoonful of sugar. Heat half-pint of new milk and before it reaches boiling point pour on the beaten egg, stirring briskly.

An excellent nourishing drink for a delicate stomach.

REDRUTH W.I. CENTRE.

EGGY'OT (1)

Heat 1 quart beer in a saucepan. Beat two eggs with two tablespoonsful sugar and add the beer when boiling.

PERRANPORTH W.I.

EGY'OT (2)

Whisk eggs to a froth, pour on hot ale and sweeten to taste.

PENPONDS W.I.

ELDER SYRUP

Put 2 or 3 quarts of elderberries, picked from the stalks, into a stone jar, set it in the oven with a plate on top. Keep pouring off the juice as it flows, then turn the berries into a sieve with piece of muslin laid in it, gather the ends of the muslin together and squeeze the berries. Put the juice into a preserving pan with 1 lb. of powdered loaf sugar to each quart of syrup and 8 cloves, and let it boil up; then heat by the fire for ¼ hour longer—it must not boil longer or it will be too thick. When cold, strain, put into small bottles, cork and keep in a cool place. Cover corks with resin.

ST. AGNES W.I.

A BIRD IN THE HAND IS WORTH TWO IN THE BUSH

TO MAKE ELDER WINE

Take a peck of elderberries, prick them and put them in an earthen pan; let them lye a week, stirring them once or twice a day, then let ye juice run thro' a range, but not squeeze it, then to a quart of ye Liquor, add two quarts of water; let it just boyle and scum it, then to every quart of that liquor put half a pound of powder sugar and boyle it a little while, stirring it, then pour out to coole it, then take a brown tost and spread it over with barm and putt into it, let it stand awhile to ripen it, then put it up into a steane or barrell and lett it stand three weeks, then draw it into bottles with a little sugar.

Dated 1727.
PENZANCE.

WHITE ELDER WINE

To a quarter-peck of elder flowers from a tree that bears white berries; allow 18 lbs. white powdered sugar, 6 gallons water and the well-beaten whites of 2 eggs. Boil these latter ingredients together and remove scum before adding the elder flowers, taking off the fire before doing so. When nearly cold, stir and add 6 spoonsful lemon-juice and 4 ozs. yeast. Beat these well into liquor, and stir it every day for 3 days. Put into cask with 6 lbs. stoned raisins, and tun the wine. Stop it close and bottle in 6 months. This wine will keep for years.

BOSCASTLE.

ELDERBERRY WINE

To every quart of berries allow 2 quarts of water. Boil together for half an hour, pour off the liquid and press the berries through a sieve. Add this pulp to the liquid and to every quart of juice put ¾ lb. coarse sugar. Boil the whole quarter of an hour with a few peppers, cloves, and small piece of ginger. Pour into a vessel with four teaspoonsful of yeast to work. When it ceases to hiss, put 1 quart brandy to every eight gallons of liquid and stop up. Bottle about Christmas time. The liquor must be kept in a warm place to make it work.

BOSCASTLE.

EVER DRUNK EVER DRY

GILLIFLOWER WINE

To three gallons of water put six pounds of the best powder sugar; boil the sugar and water together for the space of half an hour, keep skimming it as the scum rises; let it stand to cool. Beat up three ounces of syrup of betony, with a large spoonful of ale-yeast, put it into the liquor, and brew it well together; then, having a peck of gilliflowers, cut from the stalks, put them into the liquor, let them infuse and work together three days, covered with a cloth; strain it and put it into a cask and let it settle for three or four weeks, then bottle it.

ST. STEPHENS W.I. 1753.

GINGER WINE

Take 2 gallons of water, 6 lbs. of sugar, a quarter of best ginger cut in small pieces. Boil the sugar and water together till the scum is entirely taken off, then put in the ginger and boil the whole gently for half an hour, pour the liquor boiling hot on the peels of 12 lemons.

When cold put in the juice of the lemons and 3 spoonsful of new barm into the barrels with it. Let it work two or three days, then put in half-pint of brandy and close up the barrel. It would be better to put some raisins in the barrel.

MAWGAN-IN-MENEAGE.

This has been made by the same family for many generations.

HARVEST DRINK

Put ¼ lb. fine oatmeal to 6 ozs. sugar and half a lemon, cut into slices. Mix all together in a pan with a little warm water, then add one gallon boiling water and mix thoroughly. Strain, and use as soon as it is cold.

BOSCASTLE.

LINSEED AND LIQUORICE TEA

Ingredients:
    2 qts. boiling water   12 drachms liquorice root, sliced
    1 oz. whole linseed
    A few slices of lemon

Method: Pour the boiling water on the linseed and liquorice. Stand for 6 hours, then strain. Excellent for Coughs.

SUMMERCOURT W.I.

A GOLDEN KEY OPENS ANY GATE

MAHOGANY—A CORNISH DRINK

A mixture of two parts gin and one part treacle, well beaten together.

SUMMERCOURT W.I.

At a dinner given by Sir Joshua Reynolds on March 30, 1871, when Dr. Johnson and Boswell were among the guests, Mr. Eliot of Port Eliot mentioned a curious liquor peculiar to his county which the Cornish fishermen drink, made as above, and at Boswell's request Mr. Eliot " made some with proper skill," and it was greatly appreciated.—SIR ARTHUR QUILLER-COUCH.

METHEGLIN (1)*

4 lbs. honey, 1 gallon water, boil it one hour; skim well, then add 1 oz. hops to every gallon; boil it half an hour longer, and let it stand till next day. Put it into a cask or bottles. To every gallon add 1 gill brandy. Stop it lightly till fermentation is over, then stop it close; keep one year before use. Those who preferred the flavour, and perfume of aromatic plants such as thyme, rosemary, sweet-briar and heather, boiled them in the water before adding the honey. It was never considered good till three years old.—From *Bottrell's* "WEST COUNTRY LEGENDS."

I may add that my Father brewed it from Honey, Heather, and roast Apples.

J. C. H., MADRON.

METHEGLIN (2)

To every quart of Honey put a gallon of water, boyled about an hour before you put in ye Honey, then boyle both together about an hour more, and scrum it clean, then put in a bag, Ginger, Nutmeg, Cloves, Mace and Cinamon, sufficient for this quantity. When 'tis cold enough you may put two spoonfuls of new yest and put in ye Vessel to work a little. To be sur 'tis strong enough trye it when ye honey is melted, if twill bear an egg, if not, add more Honey, put ye bagg of Spice into ye Vessel to remain tyed to a string to hang about ye middle of ye barrell with a Stone to keep it from Swimming.

PENZANCE.

Dated 1727.

---

* Metheglin is probably derived from the Welsh medd (mead) and llyn (liquor). It was apparently a favourite drink some 60 or 70 years ago, generally given hot to " speed the parting guest."

METHEGLIN (3)

Metheglin proceeds from the Improvement of Bees, and thus it is made, viz., after the Honey is draines from the Combs as much as may be, they steep them in a small Wort made of Malt and Water, and press out the remaining sweet through a Bag, the Wort being cold, then they add several handfuls of Rie Meal, and a pint of new Milk to each Gallon, being first curdled posset-wise, and the Curd taken off them; adding more Honey, they boil up the Wort, and so draw it off into Casks, where, being settled and well purged, it is again drawn off into Bottles and kept for use, being very cool and pleasant.

PENZANCE.

Dated 1698.

METHEGLAN

For one gallon of Metheglan allow 3 lbs. honey in the comb (old honeycomb preferable), 2 ozs. whole ginger, 1 oz. barm (yeast), and water. Put honeycomb in pan with enough cold water to cover it, let it stand 5 days, then strain; bruise the ginger and put it in a muslin bag and boil with the honey for 2 or 3 hours; take scum off until clear. Test the sweetness with an egg; if sweet enough the egg will rise to the top; if not add more honey; take off fire; when nearly cold, add the yeast, then put in bottles, keep filling bottles until it has finished working, then cork tightly.

BOSCASTLE.

This recipe has been in use at Boscastle for over 160 years.

MILK PUNCH

Steep the peel of 9 lemons (cut very thin) for 3 days in one pint of rum. Keep it closely covered. On the second day squeeze the juice of the lemons on 1½ lbs. sugar. The third day mix these together, adding three pints of rum, five pints of cold water that has been boiled, and two pints of boiling milk, stir whilst pouring in the milk. Cover it closely and let it stand for two hours. Strain through a jelly bag and bottle.

SENNEN W.I.

Dated September 3rd, 1849.

WHERE THERE'S A WILL THERE'S A WAY

NEGUS

One dessert-spoonful blackcurrant jam in a tumbler of boiling water, allow to cool. A drink for sore throats.

J. C. H.

ORGAN TEA

This tea was a very common drink, obtained from the Mint family (*mentha pulegium*) commonly called Penny Royal. It was gathered in season, dried, kept in stock and used almost daily by older members of the family.

J. C. H.

PARSNIP WINE (1)

Take 15 lbs. of sliced parsnip and boil until quite tender in 5 gallons of water. Drain the liquor thoroughly from them, run the pulp through a fine sieve, return the liquor into a boiler and add 3 lbs. loaf sugar to every gallon; boil the whole for ¾ of an hour. When tepid lay a toast covered with yeast in it and cover, keeping it in a warm place, when it begins to ferment. Put it into a cask taking out the toast. It should not be racked until the Autumn, not bottled till six months afterwards.

MAWGAN W.I.

PARSNIP WINE (2)

Clean and cut 9 lbs. of parsnips into slices, and boil them until soft, in five gallons of water. Strain and press out the liquor and to each gallon allow 3 lbs. loaf sugar. Boil for ¾ hour, then cool. When lukewarm add a piece of toast spread with yeast. Leave it in a tub with a cover over it for 10 days, stirring daily. Then put it into a cask, and bung tightly when fermentation has ceased.

SHORTLANESEND W.I.

PEPPERMINT

This drink was a great favourite, and usually called Stillwater, and home-made. There were numerous stills in various parts of the County to which you could take a bundle of the herb, and from which the owner of the still would take toll.

I think it was distilled from Corn-mint, *mentha Arvensis*.

J. C. H.

FEATHER BY FEATHER THE GOOSE IS PLUCKED

POSSET

Hot milk curdled with sweetened liquor and spice. Generally a light-coloured dry wine was used.

J. C. H.

POTATO WINE

Wash well and cut in half half-a-gallon of small potatoes, put in a pan with 1 gallon of water, boil for five minutes. Have ready in a bowl 3 lbs. Demerara sugar, the rinds of three oranges and two lemons sliced. Pour the boiling liquor over this through a strainer. Stir well and return the liquor to the pan, adding two or three pieces of bruised ginger, and boil for half an hour. Strain into pan and leave until next day. Then bottle, but cork lightly until the working has stopped. Put a little sugar candy in each bottle and store for six months.

Falmouth W.I. Centre.

RHUBARB DRINK

Wash and slice enough rhubarb (carefully wiped and peeled) to fill a pint measure. Add a small teacupful of scalded pearl barley, and a bit of bruised ginger. Cook with five pints of cold water, in a stone jar in a slow oven for three hours, and sweeten. Put enough sugar to make it pleasant to the taste, yet not so sweet as to destroy the acid flavour of the rhubarb, which is most wholesome for the blood.

St. Agnes W.I.

SAMSON

Allow one pint of cider to half-pint of rum, boil together for one hour, then, when cold, bottle. Quantity to take a wineglassful, sweetened to taste with honey.

Boscastle.

SHANDY-GAFF

This drink is considered splendid for colds, and has been known to be made in the Boscastle district since the 17th century.

One part beer; one part ginger-beer.

J. C. H.

SHE-NAC-RUM OR CHE-NÁ-GRUM

Hot beer, rum, sliced lemon, nutmeg, sugar (sometimes ginger). Favourite Christmas drink.

J. C. H.

SHENAGRUM

Take 2 lumps of sugar, 1 wineglass of rum, 2 slice of lemon with rind. Fill the glass with boiled beer.

St. Agnes W.I.

THEY THAT CAN'T SCHEMEY MUST LOUSTER

BEVERAGES

SHRUB

A drink made of sweetened fruit juice, and although considered a temperance drink spirit is sometimes added; but generally diluted with hot or cold water.

J. C. H.

SLOE GIN (1)

Two quarts gin, 1 quart sloes (pricked with a needle). Sweeten to taste with sugar-candy (broken). Roll jar at intervals and bottle after being made about 12 months.

TREVELLAS W.I.

SLOE GIN (2)

To every quart of sloes add one quart of water; soak together until they begin to mildew, then strain off the liquid while it is clear, and boil. Add one pound of loaf sugar to every quart of liquor, add also a small quantity of ginger, or spice if preferred. Boil from ¾ to 1 hour. When cold add ½ pint gin to every quart of liquor. When it has finished working put into bottles. A few of the kernels cracked up improves the flavour.

BOSCASTLE.

SLOE WINE

One pint boiling water to one pint of sloes, stand for eight days, stirring every day, then strain and add one pound of loaf sugar to every quart of wine; then bottle.

PADSTOW.

SPRUCE

One lb. lump sugar, dissolved in hot water, to which add 2 teaspoonsful tartaric acid, a teaspoonful ground ginger, 15 drops essence of lemon; then add cold water until you have 1 gallon with ingredients.

SAINT ISSEY AND LITTLE PETHERICK W.I.

An old Cornish harvest drink.

SWEET DRINK

The old-fashioned name for Metheglin. Bottles were filled with it, stood in a window of the pantry, and an ear of barley stuck upside down in the neck of each bottle to ferment it.

MULLION W.I.

WHERE BEES ARE THERE IS HONEY

MISCELLANEOUS

BARM (1)

Put two handfuls of hops into a bag into two quarts of cold water and boil the whole for half an hour. One handful each of salt, flour, moist sugar, two or three boiled potatoes (mashed); make this into a batter with one pint of barm; when the hop water is about luke-warm, mix altogether and put in a warm place to work one night. In the morning skim and bottle, when it will be ready for use.

St. Just W.I.

BARM (2)

Ingredients:
 Tablespoonful of flour Tablespoonful of sugar
 1 potato, boiled and mashed

Method: Squeeze potato, flour and sugar together, then add warm water enough to make a good size bottleful; put three or four raisins in to make it ferment; cork bottle firmly, leave two or three days before using.

St. Just W.I.

FLOURY MILK

Bring some scalded milk to the boil and stir in thickening made of white flour and a good pinch of salt, just as for white sauce. When boiling, sprinkle in some currants and rolled spice, and slightly sweeten with sugar. Pour into basins over small squares of bread.

This was always the correct breakfast on the day when the Great Wheat Stack was carried.

Mullion W.I.

CORNISH BARM

Put 1 gallon of water in a saucepan; when boiling put in 1½ ozs. hops. Let it boil one hour. Add ¾ lb. malt and put it in a cool place. In a large basin put ¼ lb. coarse sugar, mix well with ½ pint stale barm. When what is in the saucepan is *luke warm,* strain it into the basin, stirring well. Leave it in a warm place for ten hours. Then pour it into a jar and cork. It is then fit for use.

St. Tudy.

WOMAN'S WORK IS NEVER DONE

MISCELLANEOUS

PICKLED BUTTER

Half fill a jar with cold water, add salt enough to float a good sized potato. Wrap the butter in muslin (1 lb. or ½ lb.) and put into the brine. Place a plate with a stone on top of the jar to keep the butter under the brine.

PERRANPORTH W.I.

TO PICKLE PORK, HAMS AND BACON

First go-off be sure you get a healthy pig. Don't buy one from a farmer who expects his sows to keep themselves on whatever they can pick up around the fields and hedges. So, having got your healthy pig, you feed it from the dairy all you can, and keep it in a good condition all the time. This makes a great deal of difference later in the quality of your pork.

Now we will suppose all the unpleasant part of the work is done—you have had liver for supper and liver for breakfast; it was very nice, but you don't want any more. You are ready to tackle the cutting-up and salting away.

You no doubt have assistance for the heavy part of cutting and weighing the separate quarters, but let the salting be your own particular care. Cut up your salt, 14 lb. for a pig weighing 12 to 14 score is a good allowance —mix in 5 or 6 lbs. of moist sugar and two penn'orth of saltpetre. Have a cool or half a barrel clean and dry; sprinkle a layer of salt on the bottom and lay the well-rubbed hams in first following up with the shoulders and larger pieces of pork and bacon; well sprinkle the salt mixture in all cracks and crevices. Smaller pieces leave till last and after a week these can be taken out and hung up to dry. The hams should be turned, and the brine—which will make itself—occasionally poured over the dry parts. In four weeks take up and allow to drain, then hang in bags near the stove or in any dry place.

ST. KEA W.I.

GERTY GREY

Flour and water boiled together but kept quite thin, season with salt and pepper. Eaten hot.

TREGOTHNAN W.I.

A BLACK HEN LAYS A WHITE EGG

GERTY MILK *

Flour and milk boiled together but kept "runny," season with salt and pepper and eaten hot.

TREGOTHNAN W.I.

POTATO JOWDLE

Cut up enough raw potatoes to fill a frying pan. Cover with water, add a chopped onion, pepper and salt, and fry till soft.

N.B.—A very good supper dish.

ST. COLAN W.I.

TO PICKLE SAMPHIRE

Pick it, and lay it in a strong brine of water and salt, cold; let it lie twenty-four hours, then set it on a quick fire; make it boil once, then take it up quickly, and pour it on to the Samphire; let it stand twenty-four hours, then set it again on a quick fire, and make it just boil; then take it off quickly, and let it stand till cold; then unstop it, and take it up to drain; lay it into a pot, and let the pickle settle, and cover it with the clear of it; let it stand in a cool, dry place, and if the pickle mothers, boil it once a month and let it stand till cold, and then put the Samphire to it.

PENZANCE W.I.

This is dated 1738.

SAUSAGES

Ingredients:

3¾ lbs. ham or fairly lean pork
¾ lbs. bread crumbs
Tablespoonful salt

2 tablespoonsful pepper
2 tablespoonsful thyme, chopped fine

Method: Put pork through the mincing machine, mix well with bread crumbs, salt, pepper, and thyme. Either put whole mixture through sausage machine, or make into sausages with well-floured hands.

SKY-BLUE AND SINKERS

Into a three-legged "crock" fixed over a brisk fire of furze and turf, was poured a quantity of water. While this was reaching boiling-point, some flour, usually barley,

---

* This is a breakfast dish and used in place of porridge or bread and milk by many people at the present time.

Arising from these there are two old Cornish sayings:

If a man was hacking old stumps he would say: "Gerty grey, if you won't come up, there you may stay"; or "Gerty milk, if you won't come up, I'll break the hilt."

MISCELLANEOUS

was mixed in a basin with scalded milk. This was emptied into the water in the " crock " and allowed to boil for a minute or two. Next it was poured into basins into which " sops " of barley bread had been put. These " sops " sank to the bottom, nothing being visible but the liquid, light blue in colour—hence the sobriquet " sky blue and sinkers." It was eaten with an iron spoon.

SOUR MILK

A pan of new milk would be made sufficiently warm to soon turn sour. When well set, the curd was cut across in 3 or 4 inch squares to drain off the whey. This was a real treat to many of the village folk who liked large plates full of the curd with sugar or treacle and cream.

MULLION W.I.

A TANSEY

Ingredients:

7 eggs	Cream
Tansey juice	Spinach juice
Little sugar	$\frac{1}{4}$ Naples biscuits
Nutmeg	White wine (1 glass)

Method: Beat the eggs, yolks and whites sparately; add $\frac{1}{4}$ pint cream, some of the spinach juice and small quantity of tansey juice, the Naples biscuits, sugar to taste and the white wine, a little grated nutmeg. Put all in a saucepan just to thicken over the fire. Line a pie-dish with pastry, pour in the mixture, and bake to a nice brown.

BOSCASTLE.

TOAD-IN-THE-HOLE (1)

Ingredients:

2 breakfast cups of flour	1 teaspoonful vinegar
1 teaspoonful baking powder	1 pint milk
	3 eggs
	1 lb. sausages

Method: Pour the milk into a bowl and well whisk in 3 eggs with a pinch of salt and the vinegar; then handshake in the flour and baking powder very lightly, beating all the time. Pour into a well-greased, flat baking tin and arrange sausages on top of batter. Well pricked steak could be used instead of sausages, if preferred. Time, $1\frac{1}{2}$ hours in a nice oven.

SHORTLANESEND W.I.

BETTER HALF AN EGG THAN AN EMPTY SHELL

TOAD-IN-THE-HOLE (2)

Take a piece of pastry, roll it into a round the size of a dinner plate, keeping the pastry fairly thick—about ½ inch. Then lightly mark out a round with a small tea plate. Slip your knife flat under this round about ¾ of the way back being careful not to cut the flap right off. Then lift back this flap of pastry, and put a piece of steak into the hollow, turn the pastry back over the meat, after adding pepper and salt and a little water, and bake in a fairly hot oven.

LAMBOURNE W.I.

TOAD-IN-THE-HOLE (3)

Take 1 lb. mashed potatoes, ¼ lb. grated suet, flour to bind, and salt to season. Mix to a fairly stiff dough with beaten egg and milk. Roll out into a round ¾ inch in thickness. Cut the cake partly through in places, and insert rolls of ham, or fresh meat. Bake in a good oven till brown.

FALMOUTH W.I.

CHOPPED POTATO TOAD-IN-THE-HOLE (4)

Ingredients:
3 large potatoes   ¼ lb. suet
3 or 4 tablespoonsful of flour

Chop altogether, put in basin. Place a piece of steak in centre and boil from 1½ to 2 hours, or roll out mixture two inches thick and put pieces of steak or salt pork on it, roll up and bake for 1 hour. Allow one piece of meat to each person.

TRURO W.I.

UNDER-ROAST

Take some good steak, cut up in fairly small strips; pepper and salt each piece, roll up and place in bottom of roasting tin, sprinkle with flour and cover with cold water. Now cover with a layer of peeled potatoes, put in oven and bake.

TRURO W.I.

OPPORTUNITIES, LIKE EGGS, COME ONE AT A TIME

REMEDIES
MEDICAL and OTHERWISE

FOR AGUE

Take six middling pills of cobwebs or apply to each wrist a plaster of treacle and soot.

DEVORAN W.I.

FOR ASTHMA (1)

Dip thick *white* blotting paper in diluted saltpetre until quite wet; dry it, and when the person is suffering put the paper on a plate and light it; it will smoulder away and the breathing will be relieved.

DEVORAN W.I.

FOR ASTHMA (2)

Brewers' Barm was often taken to relieve difficulty in breathing.

FOR BALDNESS

(*a*) Rub the part morning and evening with onions until it is red, and afterwards rub with honey; or (*b*) Wash frequently with decoction of boxwood.

TRURO W.I. CENTRE.

OINTMENT FOR BRUISES, ETC.

Gather fresh young " French " mallow leaves. Throw out any yellowing ones. Mush them up well, bruising them with a pestle and mortar, or if not, a rolling pin on a bread board does. Get some pig's fat after a pig is killed, before the butcher adds salt to it. Mix it all well with the bruised mallow mush and keep in jars covered with dust. Smear it on bruises, strained joints, ulcers, etc. It takes out any heat and pain.

(" French " Mallow—Tree Mallows.)

From childish recollections I believe the pig's fat was boiled down and the " mush " added on, but my informant did not say this. Also I do not know how long this ointment would keep good.

PERRANUTHNOE W.I.

ONE MAN'S MEAT IS ANOTHER MAN'S POISON

A DEEP BURN OR SCALD

(a) Apply the inner rind of elder well mixed with fresh butter. When this is bound on with a rag plunge the part into cold water.

(b) Mix lime-water and sweet oil to the thickness of cream and apply with a feather several times a day.

Dated 1750.
TRURO W.I. CENTRE.

CIDER AS A MEDICINE

Cider was a great stand-by in the home treatment of asthma.
MULLION.

FOR A COLD IN THE HEAD (1)

Steam of warm water alone, or of water in which elder flowers or some other mild aromatic herbs have been boiled generally affords a speedy relief.
PENPONDS W.I.

FOR A COLD IN THE HEAD (2)

Pare very thin the yellow rind of an orange, roll it up inside out and thrust a roll into each nostril.
DEVORAN W.I.

FOR COLDS

Pick Elder blossom and Angelica leaves. Steep in boiling water 10 minutes and strain. Sugar to taste.
POLKERRIS W.I.

TO REDUCE CORPULENCE

Use a vegetable diet. Breakfast and sup on milk and water (with bread) and dine on turnips, carrots or other roots, drinking water only.
TRURO W.I. CENTRE.

TO CURE COUGH

Cut pieces of brown paper to fit throat and far down front and back as cough hurts. Warm paper, cover side which is to go next to the skin with a layer of lard. Tie on to patient.
ST. JUST W.I.

FEED A COLD, BUT STARVE A FEVER

REMEDIES (MEDICAL AND OTHERWISE)

FOR COUGHS AND COLDS

Gather elder leaves and flowers on a hot day when the flowers are "full set" and the sun's at its height. Lay them on newspaper in a sunny place to dry. Tie them up in bundles or in large paper bags and hang them "from the cockage" (?) till required.

When needed take a small handful of leaves and flowers (strip the "stemmage" off), put them in a jug and pour a pint of boiling water on them. Leave them to steep for 6 or 12 hours. The liquor should then be a dark brown. Pour out half a cupful and add hot water to warm it. A spoonful of honey to it soothes sore throats, or sugar if the taste of the elder is not fancied. The same leaves can be used again with more boiling water until the liquor is only a pale yellow. Be careful to keep the "drees" out of the cup.

PERRANUTHNOE W.I.

ELDER OIL, FOR CUTS, BURNS AND SCALDS

Pick elder flowers. Tie down in a very large jam jar or sweet bottle with wide top. Place *in the sun.* Fill up to replace shrinkage. When all oil has oozed out strain into bottle. Will keep years. Smarts, but heals. Rub on gently.

POLKERRIS W.I.

EMBROCATION

Ingredients:
- 1 noggin turpentine
- 1 noggin vinegar
- 2 new-laid eggs
- A pennyworth of camphor

Method: Beat up the eggs first, then add the camphor, vinegar, and turpentine. Mix all together in a wine bottle, shake well, cork and tie down.

NANCLEDRA W.I.

This recipe is over 100 years old.

GRANDMOTHER'S EMBROCATION

Ingredients:
- ½ pint white vinegar
- ½ pint turpentine
- 2 squares camphor
- 2 new-laid eggs

Method: Mix vinegar and turpentine together, shred camphor and add the eggs whole, then beat together until

---

BETTER WAIT ON COOK THAN ON DOCTOR

creamy. Put in bottles, allowing room for shaking. It will keep any length of time. Is splendid for rheumatism or stiff joints, or cold on the chest. Rub well in till it glows.

KILKHAMPTON W.I.

FOR GOUT IN ANY LIMB

Rub the part with warm treacle and then bind on a flannel smeared therewith. Repeat this, if need be, once in twelve hours.

TRURO W.I. CENTRE.

Dated 1750.

HAIR-WASH

Camomile liquor is an excellent hair-wash, especially for fair hair. Two pints of boiling water to 3 handfuls of dried flowers and used after the first dirt is "rensed out."

PERRANUTHNOE W.I.

HERBS

Every housewife kept herbs in bags, bunches, or bundles, hanging from the rafters in an outhouse. They were relied upon for all sorts of complaints of man and beast.

MULLION W.I.

FOR HOARSENESS

Rub the soles of the feet before the fire with garlic and lard well beaten together.

DEVORAN W.I.

FOR INFLAMMATION

"French" mallow leaves, bruised and steeped in boiling water, and then laid on any inflammation, draws out the heat and pain. Ulcers and abscesses, etc., can be bathed with the liquor.

PERRANUTHNOE W.I.

CURE FOR INFLAMMATION OF THE BLADDER

Get some dried elder leaves. Steep a good handful in a jug of boiling water, after first washing them.

SENNEN W.I.

This is also a good remedy for coughs and colds.

LIGHT SUPPERS MAKE LONG DAYS

REMEDIES (MEDICAL AND OTHERWISE)

TO CURE THE OPHTHALMIA OR ANY VIOLENT INFLAMMATION

A small teaspoonful of powdered alum, *very completely* mixed with the white of an egg, and a linen rag doubled six or eight times and dipped in cold water, on which spread a little of the mixture and apply it to the *closed eye*. Repeat the application every 3 or 4 minutes, *remembering always* to dip the rag in cold water (or the alum would be too powerful) until the inflammation abates, which it invariably does in an hour or two.

KILKHAMPTON W.I.

A GOOD LINIMENT

Ingredients:
- 1 pint wine vinegar (white)
- 1 pint turpentine
- 1 pennyworth tincture of myrrh
- 1 pennyworth stick camphor
- 1 pennyworth spirit of camphor
- 2 good ducks' eggs

Method: Break the eggs and put them into a bottle with the vinegar, turpentine, etc., and shake well; when mixed it will be thick and white.

GERRANS AND PORTSCATHO W.I.

This is a very old-fashioned embrocation.

TO MAKE ELDER OINTMENT

Take a pint glass and fill it with elder blossom pickt clean from ye Stem, and then pour in some of ye best meat oyle, and fill ye Glass and lett it stand against a sunny window for a fortnight, and so keep it for use. 'Tis good for a strain or ach or bruise, use it cold by chafe it in by ye fire. Ye flowers must not be strained offe.

PENZANCE.

1727.

THE PLEURISY

Take the core of an apple, fill it with White Frankincenes, stop it close with the piece you cut out and roast it in ashes. Mash and eat it. An infallible remedy.

TRURO W.I. CENTRE.

AN APPLE A DAY KEEPS THE DOCTOR AWAY

REMEDIES (MEDICAL AND OTHERWISE)

REMOVAL OF FISH BONE

To remove a fish bone from the throat, cut a lemon in half, and suck the juice slowly. This will soften the fish bone and and give instant relief.

St. Mawgan W.I.

CURE FOR RHEUMATISM (1)

Make a silk bag and get two pennyworth of tarred twine and twist it up, put it in the bag and wear it near the spot that hurts and it will cure it.

Perranuthnoe W.I.

CURE FOR RHEUMATISM (2)

Ingredients:
- ½ pint white wine vinegar
- ½ pint spirits of turpentine
- Whites of 3 eggs
- Alum the size of a nutmeg

Makes 1½ pints.

Method: Put all in a bottle together and shake well. No cooking.

Polkerris W.I.

AIDS FOR RHEUMATIC TENDENCIES

Camomile flowers, gathered when "full faced" and in "high sun" then dried, can be used the same way as tea-leaves, i.e., boiling water poured on them, and the resulting liquor drunk instead of tea; this is good for rheumaticky folk.

Or two good handfuls of the flowers (and leaves) can be steeped in boiling water, and the rheumaticky joints bathed with the hot liquor, and the flowers made into a "plack" and bound round the inflamed joint.

Perranuthnoe W.I.

SCIATICA

Boil Nettles till soft; foment with liquor, then apply the herb as a poultice.

Has cured a Sciatica of 45 years' standing.

Truro W.I. Centre.

Dated 1750.

EAT SLOWLY, LIVE LONG

TO CURE SCIATICA

Carry a nutmeg in your hip pocket, or a potato until it withers and the sciatica will be cured. This is still done and vouched for by a reader.

REMEDY FOR STYE ON THE EYELID

Make a pack of boiled tea-leaves in a bit of clean muslin. Put it well up against the stye and keep it fixed with a bandage. Make a fresh one three times a day, if still needed. If it sticks to eyelid wash it off with luke-warm tea. Two or three days will cure the stye.

Perranuthnoe W.I.

FOR TOOTHACHE

Lay roasted parings of turnip, as hot as my be, behind the ear.

Devoran W.I.

CURE FOR WARTS

Put a lump of washing soda in an iron spoon. Thrust the spoon through the bars of the "slab" till the soda is "well swizzling," then drip the boiling soda on the heart of the wart. Two applications cure even long standing warts. If the wart be on the face where one would "flinkie" fromthe boiling soda, keep a lump of soda in your bedroom and rub it two or three times a day, moistening soda with spittle.

Perranuthnoe W.I.

FOR WHITLOWS, ETC.

Take a piece of butter, and add as much salt as you can possibly *work* into it. Apply this to the *finger* or part affected.

Kilkhampton W.I.

FOR WOUNDS

(a) Apply juice or powder of Yarrow (infallible); or (b) Bind the leaves of Ground Ivy upon it; or (c) Bind leaves of Wood Betony upon it.

This quickly heals even cut veins or sinews and draws out thorns and splinters.

Truro W.I. Centre.

BETTER KEEP CLEAN THAN MAKE CLEAN

A FEW OLD CORNISH REMEDIES

Rope-yarn is worn around the legs and wrists for rheumatism and cramp.

Boiled currants are taken at a last resource in constipation.

Hot, roast onion is placed in the ear, for a relief of earache.

New RED flannel is worn for sore throat or pains.

A recent bruise of the scalp from blow or fall, termed a " buffoon," treated by the application of the convex side of a tablespoon.

For the following remedies I am indebted to Mr. W. H. Paynter, Recorder, Callington Old Cornwall Society.—E.M.

TOOTH-ACHE

Hold a slice of apple lightly boiled between the teeth.

BLEEDING OF THE NOSE

Drink quantities of whey every morning, and eat plenty of raisins.

FOR A PAIN IN THE SIDE

At bed-time, take a fresh cabbage leaf, hold it to the fire until it is quite warm, and then apply it to the part affected, binding it tight with a cloth round the body; let it remain for twelve hours or more, when it will generally be found to have removed the pain; it will be well, however, to repeat the application of a fresh leaf on taking off the first, and let it remain as before. This will seldom fail in its effect.

NETTLE RASH AND STING OF A NETTLE

Rub the parts affected strongly with parsley.

COLD IN THE HEAD

Boil a handful of rosemary in a quart of spring water. Put it in a jug and hold your head, covered with a cloth, over the steam as hot as you can bear it.

GLUTTONY KILLS MORE THAN THE SWORD

REMEDIES (MEDICAL AND OTHERWISE)

BLISTERS

Blisters on the feet, occasioned by much walking, can be cured by drawing a needleful of worsted through them; clip it off at both ends, and leave it till the skin peels off.

EAR-ACHE

Place in the ear a roasted fig, or onion, as hot as may be.

CHIN-COUGH (WHOOPING COUGH)

Rub the feet of the sufferer thoroughly with pig's lard, before the fire, at going to bed, and keep the sufferer warm therein.

CHILBLAINS (1)

Apply a poultice of roasted onions hot. Keep it on three or four days if not cured sooner.

CHILBLAINS (2)

Squeeze out the juice of a leek and mix it with cream, and cover the chilblains with it.

CORNS (1)

Apply fresh, every morning, the yeast of small beer spread on a rag.

CORNS (2)

After paring them close, apply bruised ivy-leaves daily, and in fifteen to twenty days they will drop out.

FOR AGUE (1)

Slit a large onion and apply it to the stomach.

FOR AGUE (2)

Take a handful of groundsel, shred it small, put it into a paper bag four inches square, pricking that side which is next to the skin full of holes; cover this with a thin linen, and wear it on the pit of the stomach, renewing it every two hours until well.

DIET CURES MORE THAN THE DOCTOR

A CORNISH OVEN

A CLOME OB'N AND A "BAKER"

You ask me to write and tell you what a " clome ob'n " is like. Well, 1 will do my best.

I take it that you never saw one. That is a pity, for I dunno which will be the hardest, to describe it or to imagine it from the description. You must know that years and years ago, before Watts, his name, invented steam, or coal mines were discovered, that people still ate bread, at least, perhaps not so much as they do to-day. I believe they used to eat more oatmeal, and more " fry teddies;" still what bread there was had to be baked somehow, and I believe the first and oldest way of baking bread, or anything else, was by means of a " flat ire " in the open chimbley.

I have baked on it scores of times before we had one of the new fashioned " apparatusus," and my mother never baked on nothing else, except in the " clome ob'n." We only heated the latter for a big baking, say once a week or so.

The " flat ire " was " etted up " quicker, and was plenty big enough for a few pasties or a roast, or tart, or anything we might want for dinner or tay.

We first of all put the " flat ire " on the brandis (a three-legged iron affair) and then we lit a fire under it of sticks and " brimbles," furze and anything that would give a clear " ett," and after about twenty minutes or so the " ire " would white 'ot, and fire would be allowed to die down, when we would take out the brandis, and " drop the ire " (a round heavy sheet of iron with a handle at each side) among the ashes ,wipe off whatever ashes was on it, and drop our loaf of bread, or whatever we were going to bake, right in the centre. The " baker " (it looked like a huge frying-pan without a handle) was then turned over on it and red-hot ashes piled up all over and that was all there was to do.

If it was a loaf of bread it took about an hour, and lovely bread it would be, too.

Now I will try and tell 'ee how to " Ett a Clome Ob'n."

LIKE JAN TRESIZE'S GEESE, NEVER HAPPY

CORNISH OVEN, DESCRIPTION OF A

The oven (or ob'n) is simply a hole in the wall of the chimbley, there must be hundreds of them walled up in Cornwall, for every old house had one, and I daresay some have still got them.

They are oval in shape and are roofed over with a hard white substance which gave it the name of "clome." It took about an hour to "ett," and the fire had to be kept burning clear all the time the fire was *in* it of course, and at first it would all turn black, but gradually it would grow white.

Blackthorn was the favourite fuel for heating it with, and the ashes had to be kept raked out, so the bottom would get hot as well as the sides and roof. When it was white 'ot to the very door, the ashes were thoroughly cleaned out and the tins of bread and plum cake put in (our oven would hold ten tins), the door was shut and red ashes piled around it to keep out any draught, and there you were, nothing more to do till it was ready to come out an hour later, a lot less trouble and a whole lot cleaner than blackleading a new-fashioned apparatus to my mind.

St. Kea W.I.

The above was given in response to an appeal for a description of the old ways of baking bread, cakes, pasties and such like.

CLOAM OVEN

This one was built in a wall and contained a smaller one inside. To use it, it was made red hot with a fire of sticks of furze and wood. When red hot the remains of fire were raked out. Tarts and cakes were placed in the smaller, and bread under iron kettles in the larger. A gallon loaf took 1½ hours to bake. When closed the oven should not be opened until time for cooking is up.

St. Just W.I.

BAKING IRON AND KETTLE

Heat baking iron to red heat. Heat Kettle. Place bread or cake on iron, cover with kettle, surround with hot cinders and cover with burning furze and turf. Bake 1 to 1½ hours according to size.

St. Just W.I.

UNLESS THEY BE WHERE THEY BAIN'T

www.ingramcontent.com/pod-product-compliance
Lightning Source LLC
Chambersburg PA
CBHW021158080526
44588CB00008B/401